TELLURIDE IN THE

FILM FESTIVAL GALAXY

Jeffrey Ruoff © 2016

D1566109

à Natalie,

qui aura 25 ans en l'an 2026

The success of any film festival depends not on the movies that are shown, but on the guest celebrities that are lured to attend.

– James Card, co-founder, Telluride Film Festival

First published in Great Britain in 2016 by
St Andrews Film Studies
Edgecliffe, The Scores, St Andrews, Fife KY16 9AL
Scotland, United Kingdom

Secure on-line ordering:
http://www.st-andrews.ac.uk/globalcinema/publishing/catalogue

Series: *Films Need Festivals, Festivals Need Films*
Series Editor: Dina Iordanova

British Library Cataloguing-in-Publication Data
A catalogue record for this book is available from the British Library.

ISBN 978-1-908437-19-8 (paperback)

University of
St Andrews

The book is published with the assistance of the Institute
for Global Cinema and Creative Cultures at the University
of St Andrews.

St Andrews Film Studies promotes greater understanding
of, and access to, international cinema and film culture
worldwide.

The University of St Andrews is a charity registered in
Scotland, No. SC013532.

Cover design: Duncan Stewart and Jeffrey Ruoff.
Pre-press: University of St Andrews Print & Design.

Cover image: © Jeffrey Ruoff.

Inside illustrations, with permission from:
© Jeffrey Ruoff, Philip Borgeson, Stan Heller, Telluride Historical Museum,
Telluride Film Festival.

Printed in Great Britain by Lightning Source.

Contents

Acknowledgements

In a variety of capacities — as a cinéphile, as a documentary filmmaker, as a juror — I have been fortunate to attend festivals in Israel, Greece, Tunisia, Germany, Italy, the Netherlands, Morocco, Burkina Faso, Scotland, the USA, and Turkey. These festivals have given me great delight and rich intellectual exchange — with filmmakers, programmers, critics, and cinéphiles — as well as insight into international film culture.

This monograph grew out of a conversation with my film studies colleague Dina Iordanova, in Modena, Italy, where we were attending an academic conference on 'Film Festival Cartographies' at the University of Reggio Emilia in November 2014. Dina had previously published my 2012 anthology *Coming Soon to a Festival Near You: Programming Film Festivals*, a successful collaboration, which brought together the various perspectives of festival programmers, film scholars, and critics on the growing importance of festivals in film culture worldwide, a work that significantly informed my thinking here.

Having recently completed extensive research on the Colorado-based Telluride Film Festival, I presented a paper in Modena juxtaposing its first edition in 1974 with its 40th anniversary in 2013. At the conference hotel, Dina suggested that I revise my materials for a monograph on Telluride, of which this work is the result. The least studied of the major international film festivals, Telluride has a number of distinctive features that merit sustained attention. This monograph also offers an opportunity to reprint my 2012 interview with Telluride co-founders Bill Pence and Stella Pence and Brigitta B. Wagner's lively 2013 interview with co-founder Tom Luddy, bringing together the sum total of academic work on the festival. These reprinted chapters allow the co-founders to speak at length in their own words about Telluride. I especially enjoy the rich interplay between Bill and Stella, demonstrating their lifelong partnership.

Over the years, I have enjoyed discussing festivals with Bill, who has been Director of Film at the Hopkins Center For the Arts at Dartmouth College since 1983. Over the course of 2012–13, Bill and I hosted a celebration of world film festivals, bringing to Hanover, New Hampshire, the directors of the New York Film Festival, the Ottawa International Animation Festival in Canada, the Pordenone Silent Film Festival in Italy, the Busan International Film Festival in South Korea, the New York African Film Festival, and the Full Frame Documentary Film Festival in Durham, North Carolina. It was a pleasure to discuss festivals with the likes of Richard Peña, Chris Robinson, Paolo Cherchi Usai, Cho Young-Jung, Mahen Bonetti, and Sadie Tillery.

I am greatly indebted to the dozens of people I interviewed in the course of my research on Telluride, beginning with the Pences and Tom Luddy. The many others, too numerous to list here, are heard throughout the manuscript and may be found in the Works Cited section of the volume. I appreciate the assistance of the staff at the Department of Special Collections in the Margaret Herrick Library at the Academy of Motion Picture Arts and Sciences in Los Angeles, which holds the Telluride archive, and Justin Bradshaw at the Berkeley headquarters of Telluride. My thanks to the Office of the Provost, the Office of the Dean of the Faculty, and the Leslie Center for the Humanities, all at Dartmouth, for supporting for my research on Telluride.

For comments on earlier drafts of various sections of this monograph, I am grateful to my academic colleagues Rich Horwitz, Amy Lawrence, Gerd Gemunden, and Lydia Papadimitriou. The Pences graciously proofed an early draft for errors of fact. Critic and novelist Phillip Lopate, a long-time Telluride attendee and guest curator there, gave valuable feedback at the initial stages. Richard Peña, director of the New York Film Festival from 1988–2012, brought his formidable knowledge of world film festivals to the latter stages of the chapters on Telluride 1974 and 2013. Similarly, as a specialist in film festival studies, my academic colleague Ger Zielinski thoughtfully commented on these sections. Former journalist Cornelia Waterfall elegantly combed the completed work with a thorough eye and pen. I also appreciate comments I received from an anonymous peer reviewer solicited by St Andrews Film Studies.

I am grateful to my Dartmouth College undergraduate research associate Andrew Kingsley for conversation and commentary as well as our college's Junior Scholar program that supported his work. I would like to acknowledge my other students, too numerous to mention individually, whose comments have contributed to my thinking on festivals, especially those who accompanied me on a study abroad programme centred around the 2012 Edinburgh International Film Festival. The course that I taught on 'Film Festivals' there was enlivened by appearances by programmer, critic, and filmmaker Marc Cousins, film critic Gerry Peary, then-Edinburgh International Film Festival director Chris Fujiwara, and my ever-present St Andrews colleague Dina Iordanova.

I would like to single out my senior colleagues at Dartmouth — Gerd Gemunden, Amy Lawrence, Dennis Washburn, Mary Jean Green, Mary Flanagan, Barry Scherr, and David Ehrlich — for their support and the fine examples of their own scholarship and creative work. While writing this manuscript, I had the distinct pleasure of co-editing, with Lydia Papadimitriou, a special issue of the *New Review of Film and Television Studies*, devoted to 'Film Festivals: Origins and Trajectories', forthcoming in March 2016. Thanks to journal editor Warren Buckland, Lydia and I had this opportunity to learn about exciting new research on festivals.

For keeping my computers humming, I am grateful to Arts and Humanities Research Computing at Dartmouth, in particular Susan Bibeau, Robien Wymans, Zack Bennis, and Christina Hazelton as well as Peter Ciardelli, my colleague in the Department of Film and Media Studies. I appreciate the Pences sharing their images from 1974. My thanks to photographers Stan Heller and Philip Borgeson for permission to reprint their photos of Telluride 1974. I appreciate the Telluride Historical Museum for permission to reprint several photographs from their collection. All efforts have been made to contact unknown copyright holders of a handful of illustrations that appear in the monograph. Anyone with additional information about copyright should contact the author at Jeffrey.k.ruoff@dartmouth.edu.

Dina Iordanova, my editor and publisher at St Andrews Film Studies, and her assistant Andrei Gadalean, provided outstanding and judicious help throughout the whole process of manuscript preparation. I am also grateful to Dina for her elegant Foreword. The books published by St Andrews attest to Iordanova's crucial contribution to the now-established and expanding field of film festival studies. I am thankful to Dani McClellan for copy-editing the manuscript also.

My ultimate blessings, and deepest gratitude,
go to Glennis Gold, my wife, and our daughter, Natalie Gold.

'I for one, would rather see her warm supple step and the
sparkle in her face than watch all the chariots in Lydia and
foot soldiers armoured in glittering bronze.'

– Sappho, 'To Anaktoria,' 600BCE, translated by Willis Barnstone

Author Biography

Jeffrey Ruoff is a film historian, documentary filmmaker, and an associate professor of Film and Media Studies at Dartmouth College in New Hampshire, USA. In 2012, his anthology *Coming Soon to a Festival Near You: Programming Film Festivals* was published by St Andrews Film Studies. He produced and directed the documentary *Still Moving: Pilobolus at Forty* (2012) about the internationally renowned American dance company Pilobolus. In addition to writing academic articles and books Ruoff regularly publishes Op-Eds and reviews in popular newspapers and magazines, http://jeffreykruoff.tumblr.com.

List of Illustrations

Foreword

Telluride: A Bright Star in the Festival Galaxy

Dina Iordanova

For those who cherish art cinema, the Telluride Film Festival is America's best known and most celebrated film festival. It is the quintessential cinéphile film festival in the USA, and a destination festival prototype in the galaxy of festivals. It has been spoken and written about a lot in popular media, yet it has never been the subject of a monograph. This is the first study to explore Telluride's multi-faceted contributions to the cultural life of the United States and beyond.

There are many books dedicated to film festivals, usually hefty volumes that go deep into history and offer a wealth of details about cultural diplomacy, films, and filmmakers. This is perhaps the first book dedicated to a specific festival that stays short and focussed – a unique format that, I believe, has specific advantages.

These are the two features that make Jeff Ruoff's book special. It makes new research material public and, through that, it contributes to a new understanding of a venerated cultural institution. It presents all this in a new format that makes it easily adaptable to various contexts.

A prototypical cinéphile/destination festival?

Although the Telluride Film Festival started small in 1974, its ambitions were grand. Co-founded by people professionally engaged with art cinema exhibition, distribution, and preservation, the festival's standards were set high. Global film stars descended into tiny Telluride in Colorado (population then 1,000) for a four-day celebration of film art, and then kept coming back, bringing along more and more film people. Sticking to its own idiosyncratic model, which dispenses of such traditional festival rituals as red carpets, competitions, juries, press conferences, photo calls, and rigid accreditations, and which keeps the programme unannounced so that it is a surprise to audiences who have to come trusting, the Telluride team promoted an idealist 1970s egalitarianism among attendees. Yet the festival became one of the most prestigious events of its kind. Ruoff discusses how this all worked over the forty years of the festival's existence.

In the early days Telluride would show only a handful of movies, screening just one film at a time, so that everybody present could see the same film and discuss it, a perfect platform for cinéphiles to bond. The festival recognised the importance of venues, and so it capitalised on the restored vintage Sheridan Opera House, and later on other specially built venues. Its curatorial practices stood for continuity in film art and encouraged a dialogue between old and new films. Telluride screened many repertory, classic, and silent films, proportionally a much higher percentage than any other festival in the world in the 1970s. This highly acclaimed approach triggered a revival of the interest in film heritage which eventually led to the creation of specialized festivals such as the celebrated Pordenone Silent Film Festival in Italy (founded in 1982) and the acclaimed Il Cinema Ritrovato in Bologna, Italy (1986) – both of which have since become top destinations of choice for global cinéphiles.

Cannes, Berlin and Venice may be the main festival destinations for industry professionals. Telluride, which has no market attached and no official business section, was the first 'destination' festival in North America, to which the majority of its attendees would travel from out of town. Other American festivals of the era – such as the San Francisco International Film Festival (founded 1957), the New York Film Festival (1963), the Chicago Film Festival (1964), and the now defunct Filmex in Los Angeles (1971) – were principally attended by their native, urban audiences. In its early years, the Toronto International Film Festival (1976) exclusively catered to local audiences, too; still today, the vast majority of attendees at the Montreal World Film Festival (1977) are locals. The success of Telluride, which showed it is possible to attract influential and attentive audiences to far flung locations, lay the foundation for another out-of-the-way destination festival in the Rocky Mountains: Sundance, founded in 1984 in small Park City, Utah (population then under 4,000).

And even though Telluride has never spelled out any specific business agenda or industry-related ambition, Ruoff shows that it is a festival that has more clout and leverage with industry than many much bigger festivals around the globe.

In this, Telluride is unique. Indeed, it is not a traditional 'business festival' in that it does not do business the way Cannes, Busan, and Toronto do, nor is it a typical 'audience festival' in that it does not serve local, largely non-professional audiences. Yet it is a key destination on the festival calendar, attended by many industry heavyweights and adored by the audience it has developed, a highly cultured and devout group of sophisticated cinéphiles that keep coming back season after season.

Any number of cinéphile festivals – which have no business components at all – are themselves destination festivals (Pordenone and the Festival of the Midnight Sun in Sodankylä, Finland). They are attended by travelling cinéphiles, filmmakers, perhaps critics, but not by studio executives, exhibitors, distributors, and other professionals. Even the New York Film Festival is principally a metro-festival for people who live in New York City. But NYFF, commonly regarded as the most influential festival for the USA film culture – in the critical sense and closely linked to *Film Comment*, the official publication of the Film Society of Lincoln Centre, which gives NYFF a broad reach among American film critics and cinéphiles – takes place in one of the media hubs of the world, with a highly influential local audience of taste makers.

Telluride, for its part, is a destination festival par excellence – and one that has become a destination for the industry set without formally engaging in business. By dint of close ties to Hollywood, Telluride is attended (or closely watched) by art cinema distributors and by members of the Academy of Motion Picture Arts and Sciences, and it has thus become an event on a par with Venice, Toronto, and other mega-festivals. Telluride does all this without the industry trappings that turn other film festivals into complex organisations marked by a detached corporate style. It remains an audience-centric cinéphile festival, with one foot firmly planted in the industry. Its presence has transformed the fortunes of its remote location, bringing economic growth and prosperity. In that, Telluride appears to be the ultimate illustration of what James English has termed 'economies of prestige' (2008). It shows how proper attention to cultural values can have transformative power and impact.

A prototypical festival book?

It was at breakfast, over true espresso at a conference in Italy in 2014, on a breezy and glorious November day, that I persuaded Jeff Ruoff to write this book and thus explore, for the first time, what I now believe could become a model for other writing on individual festivals.

I had read or seen him present some of his work on Telluride, which I knew he had been engaged with for quite a few years, so I tried to communicate my view that he actually had enough to offer an authoritative book on the festival – a major cultural event in the United States, which nonetheless had not been explored and written systematically about so far. It was in the context of this conversation and in its aftermath that I gradually realised that it was not only a discussion about this specific book, but also on the topic of what I now believe is the most suitable format for books on film festivals.

I had read a number of books about Cannes, some on Berlinale and Venice, a book on Toronto, and I had seen many other hefty volumes about other festivals. Usually they were serious tomes with plenty of historical detail. The people who wrote them were historians who loved their sources and who would go into great detail and offer a wealth of material about the context, and about films, guests, and juries. Other festival books, usually written by journalists, were picking selected topics only and were more engaged in trying to give some sense of the feel of the festival. Neither of these kinds of books could be used, however, for the study of festivals in the context of academia, and neither was particularly instrumental in assisting our understanding of the festival galaxy at large. Unlike these books, Jeff Ruoff's study on Telluride, I believe, directly works towards the purpose of understanding festivals. In a way, it represents the ideal model of what a festival book should be in order to be of interest not only to academics, but also to students, journalists, managers, and curators – both at film festivals and beyond.

The following features, in my view, make it a model to follow when writing on other festivals.

First of all, a book like this should be short. A short book is easy to read, easy to teach, and easy to embrace. It is accessible and elegant. The argument is spelled out in a clear and captivating manner. Telluride, of course, could provide the material for a huge volume, and it surely will – one day. However, the advantages of having a concise and yet analytical study of it today are discernible.

Secondly, the book is structured around snapshots. Rather than extolling the history of the festival (now over forty years long), the book focuses on select points in its timeline – in this instance, the inaugural edition, and then another one, its 40th anniversary in 2013 – which provide abundant material for analysis and allow the author to make important observations on Telluride's exclusive features and contributions.

Third, it brings together interviews with analysis that draws on extensive references to research into film festivals in general, thus integrating the points of view of festival insiders (programmers, organisers) and outsiders (users, theorists) in a truly fruitful manner. The interviews with the Pences and Tom Luddy provide excellent primary source material for reflection about key curatorial and management decisions. These are then enriched by the analysis, informed by the author's superb command of theoretical and historical knowledge on film culture at large.

Fourth, the analysis takes the focus away from the films and concentrates, instead, on matters of organisation, venues, promotion, audiences, and stakeholders. Indeed, as I have argued elsewhere (Iordanova 2016a, 2016b), in order to understand the way a film festival operates, one of the first acts should be to switch the attention away from films. Films matter enormously, of course, but it is these other factors that must be scrutinised in order to understand what gives a film festival like Telluride its distinctiveness.

And last but not least, the short third chapter here offers a succinct summary of the specific features of the festival and thus outlines its incomparable physiognomy. It is a superior distillation of all claims made in the book and of all factual material that is presented here.

If we had more short and elegant books like this one, that followed the template I just outlined and offered such lists of specific features about more festivals, we could navigate the festival galaxy with more ease.

Chapter 1
A Festival Is Born: Telluride 1974

Opening Night

9pm. The stage is set, projectors ready. The organist who travelled to Telluride, Colorado, for this evening — Friday, 30 August 1974 — sits waiting at his instrument. The vintage Sheridan Opera House, with 232 fixed seats, overflows with 260 audience members. They have been lured by the promise of being with one of America's greatest and most legendary movie stars. Led to the stage by a teenage volunteer, Gloria Swanson, now 75, wearing a red chiffon dress and a sequinned cap, makes an impressive entrance to thunderous applause. The lights dim, silent 35mm pictures flicker on the screen, live organ music starts, and, from her stage box, Swanson begins narrating her career in silent films. She starts with Hollywood clips from 1916, when she appeared in slapstick comedies for Mack Sennett, continuing through her work with director Cecil B. DeMille, and her roles as the romantic lead in movies that made her a world-famous actress and fashion icon in the 1920s. The audience soaks up the diva's stories, jokes, and anecdotes. Afterwards, as the lights come up, James Card of the George Eastman House International Museum of Photography, presents Swanson with a Silver Medallion honouring her career. The first Telluride Film Festival has begun[1] (figure I.1).

Film Festivals and Film History

Film festivals are becoming increasingly important institutions of film culture. In 2010, at a workshop I organised at Dartmouth College — which led to the publication of my anthology *Coming Soon to a Festival Near You: Programming Film Festivals* (2012) — I asked then New York Film Festival director Richard Peña how one would write the history of the NYFF. Peña's answer was straightforward: watch the movies. In contrast to this text-specific approach, Telluride co-founder Bill Pence offered another perspective, saying that while the films screened may be the *raison d'être* for film festivals, the larger atmosphere and community should be the focus of any history. Indeed, critic Peter Cowie, in *The Berlinale, the Festival* — his capsule summary of 50 years of the Berlin International Film Festival, based on his own regular attendance over many years — hardly analyses any movies (2010). Director Satyajit Ray, recalling his time on the Berlin jury, remarks that 'Film festivals are memorable not so much for the films one sees there as for the people

I.1 The moniker of the Telluride Film Festival has always been 'SHOW', seen here outside the opera house in 1974. The term appears each year on the annual commissioned festival poster. © Philip Borgeson

one meets: directors, producers, critics, actors from all over the world' (Cowie 2010: 123-4). It is fitting that Pence and Peña had this exchange, since Telluride assumed a place in the festival landscape not unlike that of the highly curated NYFF (created in 1963), though, as will be seen, with a number of significant differences. Because of their resemblances, this chapter compares and contrasts Telluride and New York throughout, in part because the significance of NYFF itself (Kern et al 2012) is not well grasped by scholars outside the USA.

With the 'historical turn' in film studies in the 1980s and afterwards, and especially the push to understand early cinema, film historians have become more sensitive to contexts. A good deal of critical energy has been spent reconstructing and reimagining the circumstances of early motion picture exhibition and reception, particularly as they differ from subsequent eras. In works such as Rick Altman's *Silent Film Sound* (2004), more attention has been paid to the ecology of silent cinema. As movies migrate now to digital formats, handheld devices, and the like, shouldn't historians be equally attentive to the contexts of 1970s screenings, especially those at festivals? Consequently, this account of Telluride 1974 is more a historical ethnography of institution- and community-building than it is film analysis. Fortunately, the organisers kept meticulous records of the first, and subsequent, festivals.

What are the historical traces that remain of the first Telluride Film Festival? Held in the Department of Special Collections in the Margaret Herrick Library at the Academy of Motion Picture Arts and Sciences in Los Angeles, the archive of the 1974 festival includes 11 folders containing financial statements, cancelled cheques, invoices, receipts, information about film prints, letters, telegrams, programmes, fliers, press releases, press clippings, lists of pass-holders, research on tributees, sample passes, as well as a box of photographs and contact sheets. Unless otherwise noted, I have culled my facts and figures from these materials, including how many passes were sold and given away, who and how many people attended the festival, the number of press passes, attendance rates for individual screenings, costs of passes, other expenses, and budget information. As well as consulting and drawing upon this archive, I was also fortunate to interview a number of participants from the 1974 edition. These include co-founders Bill Pence, Stella Pence, and Tom Luddy, long-time Telluride staffer Jim Bedford, critic and novelist Phillip Lopate, and filmmaker Robert Gardner. Unless otherwise noted, quotes and paraphrases from these individuals come from these interviews.[2]

The Venice International Film Festival was founded in 1932 to support Benito Mussolini's fascist political fortunes, and to extend the tourist season there. The Cannes Film Festival was created in 1939 by Franco-American interests in opposition to Venice (and to extend Cannes' own tourist season). The Berlinale began in 1951 with a clear cold-war agenda (and the hope of drawing visitors to the West German city). NYFF was created within the high-art establishment of the new Lincoln Centre for the Performing Arts, putting film on a par with opera, classical music, theatre, and ballet, as Phillip Lopate suggests (2012: 16). Without an explicit political agenda or the commercial backing of a local tourism industry, the Telluride Film Festival was created in 1974 to showcase silent movies, repertory, and contemporary art cinema, in opposition to run-of-the-mill Hollywood fare. NYFF featured the same categories, but in inverse order of importance. Other influential festivals — not only Venice, Cannes, Berlin, and New York, but also Sundance, Toronto, Rotterdam, New York, Locarno, Hong Kong, Edinburgh, and Busan — have been explored in entire volumes, book chapters, and significant anniversary publications.[3] To my knowledge, there are just two chapters on Telluride in academic books, both interviews (Ruoff 2012b; Wagner 2013; reprinted here), and those who have heard of the festival probably have just passing knowledge of its origins and evolution.

The history of Telluride, and particularly of its inception in 1974, deserves to be better known. For its era, it had a number of exceptional features. From the outset, it was programmed more like a cinémathèque

— a motion picture library or archive — than most film festivals, focussed on retrospectives, rediscoveries, and archival films. While NYFF integrated classic films throughout its history — including silent movies with live musical accompaniment, as well as retrospectives — its main emphasis was always showing what it considered the 'best' 25–28 features of the current year (Lopate 2012: 32). Championing classic films, Telluride established a special niche in the film festival landscape, promoting a rediscovery of silent and classic cinema, before Hollywood studios themselves became interested in marketing classical movies through festivals (Stringer 2003b: 90). Without any sponsors to satisfy, the Telluride programmers dedicated their gala opening night to Gloria Swanson.

As film scholar Marijke de Valck suggests in her timeline of festival programming, the 1970s brought on an 'age of programmers' (2012: 29), a designation that fits the highly curated Telluride. Additionally, in the 1970s, American cinéphilia had its heyday, and Telluride was born out of this crucible. As critic Susan Sontag later reminisced, 'The 1960s and early 1970s was the feverish age of movie-going, with the full-time cinéphile always hoping to find a seat as close as possible to the big screen, ideally the third row centre' (1996: 61). At the time, there were few festivals in North America, mostly metro-festivals in cities, including the Chicago Film Festival, the San Francisco International Film Festival, Filmex in Los Angeles, and NYFF. Telluride was at the head of a wave of new North American festivals. The Toronto International Film Festival started in 1976. Serge Losique, a 'fan of Telluride' according to Jim Card (1999 [1994]: 258), founded the Montreal World Film Festival in 1977. As Bill Pence recollects, Mark Fishkin, inspired by Telluride, founded the Mill Valley Film Festival in northern California in 1978. The Utah/U.S. Film Festival started in 1978 in Salt Lake City and migrated to Park City, becoming Sundance in 1984, with Robert Redford, per Telluride co-founder Stella Pence, also taking inspiration from the small Colorado festival.

Genesis

Film festivals rely on venues, and the story of Telluride begins with an old opera house in the Rocky Mountains. In 1972, Bill Pence, a film collector and vice president of the specialised distribution company Janus Films, visited Telluride, together with his partner and spouse Stella Pence, who headed 35mm theatrical sales at Janus.[4] Together they owned and operated a number of commercial and art house cinemas in Colorado. The Pences eyed with interest a historic opera house in Telluride. Built in 1914, when Telluride was an established mining town, the Sheridan

I.2 This interior view of the opera house dates to the 1920s when the theatre was in full swing as a venue for live performance, vaudeville, and motion pictures. Photo property of the Telluride Historical Museum, all rights reserved.

Opera House had seen its share of glory days, with live performances by such celebrated stage and motion picture actresses as Lillian Gish (*Broken Blossoms*, D. W. Griffith, USA, 1919) and Sarah Bernhardt (*La Voyant/ The Clairvoyant*, Leon Abrams, France, 1924)[5] (figure I.2). By 1972, the Sheridan, like its environs, was run down. Mining, which had sustained the town for more than 100 years, was in its final days. Telluride was almost a ghost town (Lichtenstein 1975); local buildings were boarded-up, businesses shuttered. Sensing opportunities for a revival of the village, the Pences decided to purchase, restore, and open the Sheridan as a year-round movie theatre. The renovation cost some $80,000 (Webb 1974), the equivalent of $378,400 in 2013 dollars. Among other touches, a rolled-up curtain with a beautiful hand-painted scene was restored. Jim Bedford, a recent Telluride arrival, was hired as the manager of the renovated opera house. As *The Denver Post* noted, 'At age 30, Bedford is typical of many of Telluride's new residents. A college graduate (history and political science), he had been a clothing salesman, free-lance artist, TV cameraman, carpet layer and office-supplies salesman, and had knocked around the country, dissatisfied with his life's mission, until he somehow ended up in Telluride and at the Sheridan' (Secrest 1974).

The vintage opera house harboured special associations with

I.3 The restored Sheridan Opera House showcased its vintage painted curtain. Inspired by what he called a 'jewel box' of a theatre, archivist James Card suggested to Bill Pence that they host a film festival there. © Philip Borgeson

the past. In keeping with the new Sheridan's period atmosphere, as Bill Pence remembers, the first film projected in February 1973 was William Wellman's silent classic *Wings* (USA, 1927), accompanied by live music. As a year-round theatre, the Sheridan showed international classics such as *Persona* (Ingmar Bergman, Sweden, 1966) as well as current domestic films such as *American Graffiti* (George Lucas, USA, 1973), providing a mixture of art house and commercial movies (Secrest 1974). In March 1974, Bill Pence invited his friend and fellow film collector James Card, of the George Eastman House (GEH) in Rochester, New York, to present some silent prints at the Pences' theatres in Aspen and Telluride. According to Pence, Card 'brought some film prints which played in our opera house in Aspen, Colorado, and the next night in our opera house in Telluride. The programme included two silent films, *Lonesome* [Pál Fejös, USA, 1928] and a Japanese film, *A Page of Madness* [*Kurutta ippëji*, Teinosuke Kinugasa, 1926]. In Aspen, the theatre was between 50 and 100 per cent full. In Telluride, the place was jammed; all 232 seats. Of course, there was nothing else to *do* in Telluride' (Ruoff 2012b: 136).

An old hand at hosting these kinds of events, James Card was like 'the Wizard of Oz', as Jim Bedford recalls, 'he was a *showman*'. A larger-than-life figure, Card harboured a great devotion for silent cinema, having previously collaborated on revivals with, for example, NYFF. A passionate film collector, Card established the motion picture collection at GEH in

1948. In Bill Pence's words, 'Card had a romance with the old West' (Ruoff 2012b: 136), which Telluride embodied in its history and well-preserved Victorian architecture. When Jim Card saw the restored Sheridan Opera House, he was smitten. Calling it a 'jewel box of a film theatre' (1999: 258), Card suggested hosting a film festival there and Pence heartily agreed (figure I.3). They discussed bringing in a third programmer, and Card recommended Tom Luddy, the young director of the Pacific Film Archive at the University of California's Berkeley Art Museum. Like NYFF, Telluride would be a festival for cinéphiles — a festival of film appreciation.[6] In overlapping but distinctive ways, the festival directors Bill Pence, Jim Card, and Tom Luddy had dedicated their professional careers to the collection, archiving, preservation, distribution, and exhibition of repertory and art cinema. In the summer of 1974, in addition to their regular jobs, and without compensation (a situation that the Pences and Luddy say continued for many years), Bill, Jim, and Tom threw themselves into programming Telluride, while Stella managed the festival's business affairs.

Telluride, City of Gold

The landscape of a festival represents one of its principal defining features — Venice and Cannes are European coastal resorts, Berlin and New York are world historical cities. In many respects, Telluride was a peculiar choice for a film festival, a tiny village at 8,500 feet dwarfed on three sides by the 12,000-foot peaks of the San Juan Mountains. Located in a box canyon, Telluride was then more than a seven-hour drive from Denver, the closest metropolitan centre. By 1970, Telluride had just 450 residents, mostly elderly people working for the declining Idorado Mine (Lichtenstein 1975). It had limited lodging. But, in addition to its physical attractions, Telluride had a storied past.

As described by Richard Fetter and Suzanne Fetter in *Telluride: From Pick to Powder* (2001 [1979]), in 1875, a mining claim was staked along the San Miguel River, leading to the founding of the village. In the 1890s, millions of dollars in silver, zinc, lead, gold, and other ore were shipped out on the newly completed Rio Grande Southern Railroad. The population of Telluride swelled to 5,000, there were more than 25 saloons, and numerous legal brothels paid taxes into the town coffers. Millionaires lived extravagantly while immigrant miners squeezed by. Telluride became renowned as the 'City of Gold' (Barbour 2006: 7).

The fortunes of Telluride ebbed for much of the twentieth century. In the wake of the Great Depression, the population dwindled to around 500 (Fetter and Fetter 2001: 135). In 1961, for its contribution to the mining industry and its architectural significance, Telluride was named a National Historic Landmark by the USA government. In the late 1960s

I.4 Beverley Hills, California, businessman and entrepreneur Joseph Zoline (far left) invested millions of dollars in developing a Telluride ski way, which, over several decades and owners, turned the old mining town into a resort. Photo property of the Telluride Historical Museum, all rights reserved.

and early 1970s, new immigrants started arriving, a gathering influx of ex-urbanites and college graduates, people who dropped out of mainstream society to move to an inexpensive place in the mountains (Coast 1974). Telluride's setting was breathtaking, in all senses of the word. The head of the canyon featured an impressive 365-foot waterfall, Bridal Veil Falls. In the early 1970s, Telluride's 'storybook Victorian homes sold for $12,000' (Lichtenstein 1975), the equivalent of $56,760 in 2013 dollars. Like the Pences with the Sheridan Opera House, young people in their twenties and thirties opened, as Jim Bedford recollects, music stores, a radio station, restaurants, and other businesses. Empty store fronts were gradually bought up and renovated.

In 1968, a Beverly Hills businessman, Joseph Zoline, with a home in Aspen, started purchasing land in Telluride with an eye to developing a ski area. On 23 December 1972 (*Telluride Tales* 2012: 5), Zoline hosted the opening of the ski resort at his Telluride Lodge (figure I.4). By the time of the first film festival in 1974, Telluride, with a population of 1,000 (Gallo 1974c), was in the process of transformation: not yet for tourists and recreation, but no longer just a fading one-company mining town. 'We had a captive audience of disaffected hippies, alternative types; people who had moved from the cities to eke out their lives in a hard scrabble community. Most of them painfully well educated', Stella Pence remembers. 'Telluride was a town in transition, just right for a film festival' (Ruoff 2012b: 136). Telluride would become the first *destination* festival in North America, that is, one that would draw most of its audience from travelling attendees.

The Festival Directors

Successful festivals do not emerge out of thin air. The Telluride Film Festival grew out of the professional activities of its three directors, Bill Pence, James Card, and Tom Luddy, each of whom was already deeply involved with institutions of repertory and art cinema. Bill Pence brought an extensive background in motion picture exhibition and distribution, which he shared in detail. Born in 1940, Pence entered the Carnegie Institute of Technology (now Carnegie Mellon University) in 1957, eventually programmed its film society, and graduated in 1961. Soon, he started collecting 35mm prints. A few years later, in the U.S. Air Force and stationed outside Paris, France, Pence spent his weekends attending screenings at the Cinémathèque Française, where he became friendly with young French cinéphiles such as Pierre Rissient and Barbet Schroeder. Once his military service was over, Pence became vice president and part owner of Janus Films in New York City during its transition from contemporary foreign film distribution to specialisation in international classics. He pioneered a 'films in repertory' concept of distribution, including successful auteur-based 'Janus Film Festivals' that toured major cities and college towns in the 1960s and 1970s. Pence was instrumental in the creation of Janus's extensive library of classic motion picture prints (which later became the basis for the influential Criterion Collection on DVD). Relocated in Denver, Colorado, Pence, together with his partner Stella, developed a chain of more than a dozen art and commercial theatres in the Rocky Mountain region. As a film collector, distributor, and exhibitor, Bill Pence championed classic movies from the USA and abroad (figure I.5).

Unlike Pence, James Card came of age during the silent cinema era. Born in 1915, Card was first and foremost a film collector. In his personal history *Seductive Cinema: The Art of Silent Film* (1999), he brings unabashed nostalgia to the collection, preservation, and exhibition of silent cinema. Shortly after purchasing a Keystone Moviegraph projector in the 1920s,

I.5 Co-founder Bill Pence brought his entrepreneurial experiences as a distributor and exhibitor to Telluride. © Stan Heller

Card began collecting motion pictures. Eventually, he used the donation of his private collection of some 800 prints as 'bait' (1999: 116) to secure a position at the George Eastman House, and to establish a film collection there in 1948. Throughout the post-war period, Card developed extensive connections in the worlds of international film collecting and preservation, including Henri Langlois of the Cinémathèque Française. Card also cultivated contacts and friendships with a wide variety of Hollywood figures. When it occurred to Card to organise a festival in the 1950s, he suggested to the director of GEH that 'the success of any film festival depends not on the movies that are shown, but on the guest celebrities that are lured to attend' (1999: 280–1). Card's first Festival of Film Artists, in 1955, focussed on the period of American movie history from 1915–25 and brought to Rochester many renowned figures, such as stars Lillian Gish and Harold Lloyd, producer Jesse Lasky, and director Frank Borzage (1999: 284). An equally remarkable group of Hollywood personalities attended the second (and final) Festival of Film Artists in 1957, which covered Hollywood from 1926–30. Through his work at

I.6 To Telluride, co-founder James Card brought archival knowledge from the George Eastman House, as well as personal acquaintance with famous stars and directors. © Philip Borgeson

GEH, Card, as much as any individual in America, helped institutionalise cinema as an art form (figure I.6).

The youngest of the Telluride festival directors, Tom Luddy, was born in 1944. Luddy described himself as 'a film buff' in high school in New York City, where he watched repertory and foreign movies at Greenwich Village art house theatres. Then, as a student at the University of California-Berkeley from 1961–66, Luddy ran several campus film societies. In 1966, after graduating, he started working full-time at the specialised distributor Brandon Films in NYC. After a year and a half there, Luddy returned to the Bay area, where he founded and ran the Telegraph Repertory Cinema from 1968–71, and worked as an assistant to Albert Johnson, the artistic director of the San Francisco International Film Festival. Luddy organised the first major programme of the Pacific Film Archive, a complete retrospective of the work of Jean-Luc Godard, culminating with a screening of his latest work, *La Chinoise* (France, 1967), with Godard in person. Of the co-founders, only Luddy provided

I.7 Co-founder Tom Luddy brought a counter-cultural emphasis to Telluride from his years as an exhibitor and archivist in the San Francisco Bay area and at the Pacific Film Archive. © Stan Heller

a strong counter-cultural emphasis, which film scholar Thomas Elsaesser sees as characteristic of festivals in the post-1968 era (2005: 100). The PFA also hosted visits from Henri Langlois, who put Luddy in touch with Card. In 1972, Luddy and Card collaborated on a three-month screening series, 'Treasures from the George Eastman House', during which 104 silent and classic motion pictures were shown at the PFA, with extensive programme notes penned by Luddy (Card 1999: 222). While Card was in the Bay area, Luddy wined and dined him at the newly opened Chez Panisse and introduced Card to Francis Ford Coppola, Kenneth Anger, Albert Johnson, and other important figures from the northern California film scene. 'Card really loved his time in Berkeley. He had a huge ego, so he loved the attention. He had a much hipper and larger audience here than he had at the George Eastman House', Luddy recollects (figure I.7).

Institutions beget institutions. Although the Telluride Film Festival may have begun with an opera house, the three cinéphile programmers were already influential taste makers in American film culture. Their backgrounds in film societies, and the distribution and exhibition of art cinema, parallel influences that shape many festivals (Taillibert 2009: 23-28, 58-60). We see traces of Telluride's auteurist bent in the 'Janus Film Festivals' that Pence circulated in the 1960s and 1970s. Card's Festivals of Film Artists in the 1950s at GEH presaged Telluride's focus on silent cinema and famous guests. Luddy's 1968 retrospective of the increasingly politicised Godard laid down a foundation for both retrospectives and oppositional, contemporary cinema. As Bill Pence put it, Card offered expertise in classic motion pictures, Luddy brought in the future, cutting edge of cinema, and Pence was the 'entrepreneur in the middle' (Ruoff 2012b: 137). This triumvirate created fertile synergies as well as balance, similar to the earlier — but more fraught — collaboration between programmers Richard Roud and Amos Vogel at NYFF, which eventually evolved into a larger selection committee (Greenspun 2012: 51). The three Telluride programmers would bring their know-how from Rochester, Berkeley, and Denver to the small town in the Rocky Mountains, emphasising film as the personal expression of individual artists, a characteristic feature of 1970s programming (de Valck 2012: 13). Film scholar Julian Stringer describes how festivals in the 1980s and after started 'raiding the archive' (2003b: 81) to screen Hollywood classics, but the Telluride founders — archivists and collectors themselves — *were* the archive.

Programming Telluride

The distinctiveness of Telluride's programme was established quickly in exchanges among the three directors. Unlike NYFF, which was spread out over several weeks of mostly evening screenings, Telluride would be short and concentrated, taking place over Labour Day weekend in early September. It would be non-competitive, like New York, with no awards that would pit filmmakers against one another, similarly screening a small selection of movies. Telluride's four-day festival would be anchored around evening-long tributes to three important film artists, two from the past, one contemporary. Directors, stars, or major archivists would present the screenings. Unlike Venice and Cannes, there would be no red carpet, no paparazzi, no press conferences, and no market. NYFF, for its part, had no market, but taking place in one of the media centres of the world, it received extensive coverage from the outset (Lopate 2012: 21) and welcomed many New York City–based industry professionals among its audiences. Unique for film festivals, an egalitarian atmosphere would prevail at Telluride — filmmakers would be encouraged to interact freely with audience members (Andrews 1974a). There would be only one

I.8 Each of the three tributees received an outdoor seminar devoted to his or her oeuvre. Here, Francis Ford Coppola (centre) holds forth at a panel discussion with the Sheridan Hotel in the background. On Coppola's right are filmmaker Dušan Makavejev and festival co-founder Tom Luddy. © Philip Borgeson main screening at a time. Outdoor seminars, scheduled when no movies showed, would bring the festival community together to debate the screenings, increasing the emphasis on formal and informal conversation (figure I.8). Unlike many festivals, Telluride would sell passes, instead of tickets for individual screenings, which committed attendees to the festival as a whole.

Pence remembers attending the San Francisco festival regularly while Luddy was working there, and both took from SFIFF director Albert Johnson the concept of in-person lifetime achievement tributes to major historical figures in cinema, then a rarity at festivals (Wagner 2013: 234). NYFF, too, annually offered gala tributes, beginning spectacularly in 1972 with Charlie Chaplin, but these were formal black-tie events at Lincoln Center conceived of as fundraisers for donors (Lopate 2012: 28). Furthermore, tributees such as Chaplin did not stick around for the duration of NYFF to mingle with audience members as would occur at Telluride. Most festivals in the 1970s focussed on new movies, but Card and Luddy were archivists. Pence and Card, both collectors, were passionate about the history of cinema. Moreover, unlike NYFF, the small scale of Telluride would nurture a feverish atmosphere. In festivals as in real estate, location is all-important. As Pence put it, 'At Telluride, the town is the festival and the festival is the town'.

The programme came together quickly in the summer of 1974. With no submissions or calls for films, the organisers turned to filmmakers and archivists they already knew (Webb 1974). Surrounded on three sides by mountains, Telluride seemed like a good place, according to Luddy, for Jim Card to celebrate one of his favourite genres, the German 'mountain film'. Card suggested tributes to Leni Riefenstahl and Gloria Swanson, both old friends of his, as well as a programme of archival treasures from GEH (Wagner 2013: 236). Luddy recalls organising the tribute to his friend Francis Ford Coppola, then at a peak of artistic and commercial success. The organisers reached out to their colleague Henri Langlois, who delivered three programmes, rare prints from the Cinémathèque Française and two new French features. By the 1960s, Langlois was already cooperating with festivals such as NYFF, where he staged a number of important revivals (Lopate 2012: 18). Tom Luddy recalls inviting the dissident Yugoslavian filmmaker Dušan Makavejev, whom he had befriended in the San Francisco Bay area.

Looking for diversity, variety, and demanding works, the programmers scheduled silent films, classics, recent features, documentaries, and experimental films. Unlike many festivals, however, Telluride was not engaged in what film scholar Liz Czach calls 'cultural nationalism' (2004: 82), or the consolidation of national identity.

Though Telluride focussed more on American movies than NYFF, both were decidedly Eurocentric. Luddy remembers that *The Thief of Bagdad* (Ludwig Berger, Michael Powell, Tim Whelan, UK, 1940) was one of Coppola's favourites, so Tom suggested that Pence show his personal 35mm Technicolor print. Pence recalls approaching avant-garde filmmaker Stan Brakhage, also based in Colorado, while Luddy invited Kenneth Anger, who was living in Luddy's Berkeley home at the time. Similarly, Pence solicited ethnographic filmmaker Robert Gardner, from Cambridge, Massachusetts. Luddy obtained a print of *Solaris* (Andrei Tarkovsky, USSR, 1972) from the San Francisco Consulate General of the Soviet Union. With tributes to Swanson and Riefenstahl, and archival programmes from the Cinémathèque Française and the George Eastman House, Telluride 1974 was — despite the presence of Coppola and Makavejev — a festival of revivals and retrospectives. True to its historical emphasis, the auteurist festival featured motion pictures from every decade from the 1910s through the 1970s. Forging alliances from Denver, Rochester, Berkeley, and Paris, the organisers established a new institution in the Rockies that highlighted the history of cinema as a multifaceted, diverse art form. Like other major festivals in the 1970s, Telluride turned its back on commercial Hollywood film, fostering a comparatively counter-public sphere (Stringer 2008: 53), and, like NYFF, an American beachhead for European auteurs.

Publicity and Attendance at the 1974 Festival

The co-founders recall reaching out to other film professionals they were in touch with on a regular basis to attend the festival, the Pences through Janus Films, Luddy through the PFA, and Card through GEH, which led to extensive participation by art house exhibitors. Being experienced programmers, distributors, and exhibitors, they also did a good job publicising the event to the media, putting out a series of releases that garnered extensive attention. The first, dated 25 July 1974, announced the in-person tributes to 'Hollywood star Gloria Swanson and directors Leni Riefenstahl and Francis Ford Coppola' (Miller 1974a: 2). The presence of three major figures swiftly attracted attention to the festival, while the provocative Riefenstahl tribute generated immediate controversy. The release gamely skirted her affiliations with Adolf Hitler and the Nazi regime, accentuating instead her artistry and gender: 'If nothing else is remembered concerning Leni Riefenstahl's contributions to the art of film, one can dwell on the fact she was a woman director working within a culture that was probably more hostile to the woman film technician than it is today' (Miller 1974a: 5). Though true enough, few press outlets took up this proto-feminist mantle. The one thing many seemed to remember was Riefenstahl's work for the National Socialist Party on *Triumph des Willens* (*Triumph of the Will,* Germany, 1935) and *Olympia* (Germany, 1938).

Fuelled by glamour and controversy, the media attention immediately established Telluride as a festival of note, even before it began. It became known not only in specialised weeklies such as *Variety* — which printed a front page article on 7 August entitled 'Nazi-Tainted Riefenstahl Honored by Colo. Fest But "T'aint Politics", It Sez Here' (1974b) — but also in general circulation publications. Not surprisingly, given the Pences' Colorado theatre chain, the festival attracted interest from in-state publications, receiving coverage in the *Telluride Times*, the *Deep Creek Review* (Telluride), *The Straight Creek Journal* (Denver), the *Daily Sentinel* (Grand Junction), the *Camera* (Boulder), the *Durango-Cortez Herald*, the *Rocky Mountain News* (Denver), and *The Denver Post*. Ongoing press attention during and after the festival also included *The Washington Post*, *Newsweek*, the *Village Voice* (New York City), *Coast* (Los Angeles), *Filmmakers Newsletter*, and *The New York Times*. (More than 15 per cent of total attendees received free press passes.) But unlike, for example, Cannes, Telluride was not organised for the media, so it didn't create the veritable 'Niagara' of print that media scholar Daniel Dayan later saw as emblematic of Sundance and festivals generally (1997: 47).

The difficulty of travelling to Telluride meant that mostly die-hard film lovers made the journey. For the cinéphiles who could manage to get to Colorado, the festival was inexpensive. In 1974, passes cost $25 (just $10 for residents), rooms $16–17 for two people per night, and there was a $50 package tour that included a bus from/to Denver, lodging for three nights, and a festival pass (Gallo 1974a). In 2013 USA dollars, these figures would be $118 for the pass (only $47 for Telluride residents), $75-80 for nightly hotel, and just $236 for the package tour.[7] Several weeks before it started, the first Telluride Film Festival sold out. Of the 329 passes distributed, 100 went to residents, 173 to visitors, 47 to the press, and nine to guest filmmakers. A cosmopolitan out-of-town crowd joined the Telluride festivities, including film historians Richard Barsam and Vlada Petric, writer Phillip Lopate, French filmmaker Jean-Pierre Gorin, film critic Elliot Stein, Michael Webb, programming manager of the American Film Institute, and actress Julie Christie, who attended without being on the programme. A roll call of major American repertory cinema owners attended, including Larry Jackson of the Orson Welles Cinema in Cambridge, MA, Al Malmfelt of the Theatre of Living Arts in Philadelphia, Bruce Trinz of the Clark Theatre in Chicago, Sydney Geffen of the Bleecker Street Cinema and Carnegie Hall Cinema in NYC, Ben Barenholtz of the Elgin Cinema in NYC, and Theodore Pedas of Circle

Films, a chain of theatres in Washington, DC. All had vested interests in repertory and art house cinema. From the very beginning, Telluride hosted a small but influential group of taste makers in American film culture, an indispensable feature of successful festivals (Czach 2004: 82).

The Programme

Like NYFF, Telluride advanced a movement to revive silent motion pictures in 35mm with live musical accompaniment, a revelation to its youthful audience. Silent-film star Gloria Swanson's evening tribute concluded with a screening of *Sadie Thompson* (Raoul Walsh, USA, 1928), produced by and starring Swanson. The only known 35mm print, from the George Eastman House, was missing its final reel. When the movie suddenly ground to a halt, as Bill Pence recollects, James Card dramatically ascended the opera house stage to issue a rousing call for film preservation and restoration. Seizing the moment, he spoke eloquently about silent pictures lost for all time and the importance of safeguarding what remained of the history of cinema. From the beginning, and before it became fashionable at other festivals in the 1980s and after, Telluride was invested in a 'preservationist agenda' (Stringer 2003b: 82). According to the Boulder newspaper *Camera*, Card was 'responsible for the air of homage — even reverence — which was the dominant note of the festival' (McReynolds 1974).

Spread over four days, Telluride 1974 included 14 shows at the Sheridan Opera House, featuring 35mm prints of movies from the USA and Europe (mostly Germany and France), five of them silent features in addition to compilations of silent shorts. At capacity, the Sheridan had 232 fixed seats. Yet, somehow, 260 people attended Swanson's tribute, 270 crammed in for Coppola's tribute, which included a screening of *The Conversation* (USA, 1974, which had won the *Palme d'or* at Cannes in May), and the audience swelled again to 252 for the Riefenstahl tribute. As Bill Pence notes, the Telluride tributes were 'the umbrella under which the whole festival operated'. An additional 11 screenings took place concurrently in a banquet room of the Telluride Lodge, 16mm projections of four movies starring Swanson, three directed by Coppola, and four starring or directed by Riefenstahl. Drawn by the political controversy surrounding the German director, 142 people squeezed into the lodge for a midnight screening of her Nazi propaganda documentary *Triumph of the Will*, while many others were turned away (Gallo 1974). Incredibly, a midnight presentation of 'underground' films by Stan Brakhage and Kenneth Anger attracted 234 audience members. 'I don't experiment', Brakhage memorably proclaimed, 'and I hate the

I.9 Surrounded by the kinds of peaks that helped make her a star actress in the German 'mountain film' genre of the 1920s, Leni Riefenstahl, 70 years old in 1974, was the focus of intense controversy — before, during, and after the first Telluride Film Festival — for the films she made for the Nazi Party. © Philip Borgeson

underground. I'm a living room man myself' (McReynolds 1974). At its outset, Telluride put the avant-garde on a par with silent films, classic features, documentaries, and contemporary European and American art cinema, offering alternatives to mainstream Hollywood. Screenings of *Solaris*, *Anna Christie* (John Griffin Wray, USA, 1923), *Sunset Boulevard* (Billy Wilder, USA, 1952) and *The Conversation* gave the 1974 festival a brooding, dark tone.

While all festivals seek to create community (Stringer 2008: 53), Telluride encouraged a stronger sense of it than NYFF, Venice, Cannes, or most other film festivals. Because the Colorado gathering offered one principal screening at a time, each festival goer saw (more or less) the same movies over the course of the festival and took part in ongoing discussions. As Stella Pence notes, 'The Flaherty Film Seminar is the closest thing to this experience, everyone sees and talks about the same films; I like that model'. Despite the accumulated star power, Riefenstahl 'clearly stole the show', according to Stella, as audience members grappled with the form and content of her oeuvre (figure I.9). Telluride helped rehabilitate Riefenstahl's reputation as a gifted filmmaker, even as it fuelled controversy about her political legacy. The tribute screening of her mountain film *Das blaue Licht* (*The Blue Light*, Germany, 1932) received a standing ovation (McReynolds 1974). Her two-part documentary on the 1936 Berlin Olympics, *Olympia*, also struck

I.10 Leni Riefenstahl stayed away from the outdoor seminar devoted to her work, leaving the central panel chair empty at the public gathering. © Stan Heller

an enthusiastic chord at Telluride, 'whose entire population', according to *The Washington Post*, 'is devoted to mountains, kite-hanging, and [horseback] riding' (Webb 1974). However, Riefenstahl's Nazi party affiliation disrupted the reverent emphasis of the festival, raising ethical and political issues among attendees. As arguments swirled in the press, protestors came down from Denver to demonstrate against her tribute and presence (Gallo 1974b). The 15 September front page of the 'Arts and Leisure' section of *The New York Times* proclaims 'Hitler's Favorite Filmmaker Honored at Colorado Festival' (Andrews 1974d). The attempt to separate Riefenstahl's mastery of the medium from the topics of her movies, at Telluride and elsewhere, inflamed critic Susan Sontag to write her celebrated 1975 essay 'Fascinating Fascism' in the *New York Review of Books*, demonstrating the indissolubility of Riefenstahl's aesthetics and politics.

The Riefenstahl outdoor seminar, wistfully entitled 'Movies: Art or Commodity', wound up instead being a referendum on fascism in film and was notable for Riefenstahl's absence; photographs of the seminar highlight her empty chair (figure I.10). Wary of the protestors, Riefenstahl stayed away. Asked about the controversy, Gloria Swanson

I.11 Outdoors in rustic Telluride, Jim Card (left) takes a break from shaving to pose for a photograph with Bill Pence, Leni Riefenstahl, and Stella Pence. Courtesy of Bill Pence and Stella Pence. © Unknown

got 'very angry, snapping, "How long ago was that? Is she still carrying a flag around for Hitler? I don't want to discuss that. I know nothing about it. Many, many untrue things have been said about me. I'll talk about that if you want"' (*The Straight Creek Journal* 1974b: 8). Swanson was outflanked by the attention given to the German director; the Pences remember that it was hard for the Hollywood star to receive second billing. Although opinions remained divided about Riefenstahl's tribute, fellow director Dušan Makavejev summarised her career well: 'Leni was a genius glorifying the wrong cause' (*Newsweek* 1974). Telluride reaped the rewards of publicity that trailed Riefenstahl. Coming right on the heels of Telluride 1974, a controversial appearance by Riefenstahl at the Films by Women/Chicago '74 Festival at the Art Institute of Chicago was cancelled, as film scholar and critic B. Ruby Rich notes (1998: 36–38). While subsequent festival brochures show that Telluride did not court controversy in future tributes, as much as anything, the furore over Riefenstahl's participation put Telluride on the map (figure I.11). As an example of its reach, former NYFF director Richard Peña, then a student living in Brazil, read about the Riefenstahl tribute in local papers in 1974 and debated its merits with his cinéphile friends there.

A Festival is Born

Film festivals are live events, not simply a collection of movies (Ruoff 2012a: 3–4). Because they are also institutions, it is important to pay attention to programmers, venues, location, audience members, funding, and the overall experience of participants. Compared to other festivals of the time, Telluride 1974 created an egalitarian ambience. Co-founder and coordinator Stella Pence credits the thin mountain air: 'It's really hard to breathe and, in a funny kind of way, everybody gets levelled by that experience'. In the tiny town, for the most part, there was nowhere, and no reason, for anyone to hide. With no red carpet, the stars and filmmakers walked the unpaved streets of Telluride. Critics and audience members loved not only the movies, but also, as Michael Webb put it in *The Washington Post* (1974: H2), 'the moments of easy contact with the famous and the knowledgeable in the heady mountain air'. Film historian Richard Barsam, writing in the *Village Voice*, echoed these sentiments, 'It was a pleasure to mingle with Julie Christie, Dušan Makavejev, Jean-Pierre Gorin, and other festival guests without the usual hullabaloo of festival press agents and photographers' (1974: 86). *The Denver Post* reported that Coppola 'talked (over beers) with anyone who had a question or wanted to listen' (Andrews 1974c). According to *Camera*, 'Everyone fell into the routine of sleeping, eating, standing in line. It was a mostly under-thirty crowd, wearing blue jeans and hiking boots. Celebrities mingled easily with lesser-knowns' (McReynolds 1974) (figure I.12). At a time when the handful of USA film festivals took place in large cities, where such an atmosphere would be difficult if not impossible to sustain, the Telluride organisers enticed visitors to a secluded village in the Rocky Mountains, where the vintage opera house was a graceful venue for a festival devoted to the past, presaging the later 'nostalgia' for classic film at international festivals (Stringer 2003b: 86). The Sheridan helped revive the atmosphere of film presentation during the silent era. The small-town Western setting offered a considerably more casual atmosphere than NYFF's urbane Philharmonic Hall at Lincoln Center,

I.12 In the low-key atmosphere of Telluride 1974, movie star Gloria Swanson mingles with critic Elliot Stein (right) and other festival goers © Philip Borgeson

seating 2,300, or its Avery Fisher Hall with 1,000 seats (Lopate 2012: 27). The presence of a coterie of art house exhibitors enhanced Telluride's connection to the circuit of specialised American theatres, as occurs with other influential festivals (Elsaesser 2005: 91).

An ecumenical event dominated by revivals, Telluride 1974 offered no world premières and just a few North American premières, including Makavejev's *Sweet Movie* (Canada/France/West Germany, 1974). According to the Pences, this sexually explicit political satire snuck past Denver customs officials, who managed to preview only inoffensive reels, and, according to the programme, played to an 'adults only' audience at the Sheridan. Not as divisive as Riefenstahl's work, *Sweet Movie*'s graphic collage nevertheless polarised the public: 'Some stormed out angrily, declaring it to be the worst piece of shit they've ever seen' (Shuman 1974). Others, such as Barsam, called *Sweet Movie* a 'work of genius' (1974: 86). In retrospect, the weakest section of the festival featured two French farces, recommended by Langlois and programmed sight unseen, *Les Chinois à Paris* (*The Chinese in Paris*, Jean Yanne, 1973) and *Touche pas à la femme blanche* (*Don't Touch the White Woman!*, Marco Ferreri, 1974). The Pences still marvel about showing these mediocre French movies, with no English subtitles to boot.

Notwithstanding a grant from the Colorado Council on the Arts and Humanities, which provided 7 per cent of the operating budget, the first Telluride Film Festival was an independent venture. This contrasts significantly with the largely governmental initiatives that created many European festivals including Venice, Cannes, and Berlin (Stringer 2001: 135) or the institutionalised setting of New York. Leaving aside the unpaid time donated by festival organisers and staff, the operating budget of Telluride 1974 was a modest $10,514, with a deficit of $2,534 covered by the Pences' theatre chain ($49,731 and $11,985, respectively, in 2013 dollars). 'Advertising and promotion' consumed more than 21 per cent of the expenses. Remarkably, the festival had no commercial sponsors; sales of passes covered two-thirds of the operating budget. It was, indeed, a different era. The festival was put on by the non-profit National Film Preserve, created by the directors at a time when Pence and Card hoped that abandoned tunnels and mining shafts in Telluride, with their low humidity and stable temperature, might one day store highly flammable 35mm nitrate prints (Barsam 1974: 86). *The Straight Creek Journal* speculated that the desire to create such an archive was 'perhaps the major impetus behind the festival' (Staples 1974). Although the preservation scheme never came to fruition, the festival took flight.

Writing in *Filmmakers Newsletter*, independent filmmaker Rodger Darbonne proclaimed that 'Telluride delivered with such success that its future must rank as one of the more significant film events in the world' (1974: 69). Forgoing red carpets, paparazzi, press conferences, and a market, Telluride opened with a clear vision of itself as a place where motion pictures of the past and the present could mingle. Like their predecessors at Venice, Cannes, and New York, Card, the Pences and Luddy, drawing on their own institutions and professional affiliations, had the expertise to make an ambitious festival happen. They brought together an exceptional gathering of filmmakers, exhibitors, and film buffs in a relaxed, and affordable atmosphere. Despite important similarities in programming to NYFF, the duration, location, and intimacy were principal differences, as well as the higher proportion of silent and classic movies that Telluride featured and the centrality of its tributes. With its eclectic program, Telluride 1974, like many festivals, clearly offered an alternative to the Hollywood studio system as well as a showcase for European auteur cinema in the USA. But, with its celebration of classical cinema, Telluride was not a counter-cultural festival such as film scholars have characterised Rotterdam (Elsaesser 2005: 106) or the Pesaro Film Festival (de Valck 2012: 30).

As James Card proposed, a successful festival depends as much on who attends as on what films are shown. Fostering a sense of community (even divided, as the Riefenstahl tribute suggests), Telluride's agenda was principally historical and aesthetic, more like a cinémathèque than a festival. While most festivals were focussed on new films and premières, Telluride shared silent cinema with live music with a new generation of viewers, creating a niche for a renewal of film history. This emphasis on classics presaged later, more specialised archival film festivals, as well as, from the 1980s onwards, a general 'revival at international film festivals of movies made during the heyday of the Hollywood studio system' (Stringer 2003b: 83). Akin to premières, theatrical presentations of 35mm nitrate prints of silent films offered discoveries of another kind. 1974 was an auspicious debut. As Tom Luddy recalls, 'It was a labour of love'. Within weeks plans were underway for a second festival (*Boxoffice* 1974a: W6). In the coming years, the festival would ride a wave of change that was sweeping the town, while simultaneously being itself a transformative force. Founded in the prime of cinéphilia, the first Telluride Film Festival was a monument to this passionate devotion to cinema and an inspiration to a wave of new North American festivals. An important institution of film culture, Telluride has now itself become a part of film history.

Notes

1   This account of the opening night of the first Telluride Film Festival draws on details from interviews with staffer Jim Bedford, co-founders Bill Pence and Stella Pence, as well as newspaper and magazine articles (Barsam 1974), (Coast 1974), (Gallo 1974b), (Reynolds 1974), and (Webb 1974).

2   The interviews I conducted took place in-person, on the phone, and/or over email. During these exchanges, all gave permission for their comments to be used. While I have not necessarily quoted or paraphrased from all the interviewees, each helped me form general impressions of the festival. Full citations of all interviews appear in Works Cited.

3   In addition to the Works Cited section of this monograph, for a broad overview of additional scholarship on film festivals in general, consult the regularly updated Film Festival Research Network bibliographies compiled by Skadi Loist and Marijke de Valck, http://www.filmfestivalresearch.org/index.php/ffrn-bibliography (15 June 2014). Kenneth Turan has a valuable chapter on Telluride in his book *Sundance to Sarajevo: Film Festivals and the World They Made* (2001), a useful overview of 12 festivals by a perceptive critic.

4   Founded in 1956 by Bryant Haliday and Cyrus Harvey, Jr., then owners of the Brattle Theatre in Cambridge, Massachusetts, Janus Films went on to become, though a series of different owners, a premiere distributor of art movies in the USA. Still an active distributor today, Janus retains a close relationship with The Criterion Collection, which releases prestige titles on DVD and Blu-Ray. 'On October 24, 2006, in celebration of 50 years of business, the Criterion Collection released 50 of the films that Janus distributed in a large box-set containing 50

DVDs and a 200-page essay on the history of art house films. The package was called *Essential Art House: 50 Years of Janus Films'*. Https://en.wikipedia.org/wiki/Janus_Films (28 September 2015).

5   Http://www.sheridanoperahouse.com/sheridan-opera-house/history (15 June 2014).

6   The importance of cinéphilia in the history of film festivals could hardly be overestimated. Although geopolitics and tourism greatly influenced the creation of Venice, Cannes, and Berlin, many festivals have grown out of the love of cinéphiles for the art of cinema. In her survey of festivals in France, *Tribulations festivalières: les festivals de cinéma et audiovisuel en France*, Christel Taillibert discusses the historic role of ciné-clubs and art house theatres as overlapping antecedents of festivals (2009: 23-28, 58-60). In *Film Festivals: Culture, People, and Power on the Global Screen*, Cindy Wong argues that postwar film festivals are more or less extensions of existing institutions of cinéphilia; small film journals, ciné-clubs, and art cinemas (2011: 30-37).

7   For the conversion of 1974 dollars into 2013 equivalents, I used the United States Department of Labor Bureau of Labor Statistics Consumer Price Index calculator at http://data.bls.gov/cgi-bin/cpicalc.pl, which estimates an inflation rate of 4.73 from 1974 to 2013.

Chapter 2
Telluride from Cinéphilia to the Oscars, 1974–2013

The Telluride Film Festival, which for decades carved a special cinéphile niche for itself, thanks to a strong curatorial voice and auteurist vision, has come to occupy a novel space in the film festival galaxy in the past 10 years.[1] Writing in *Sight and Sound* in 2009, film critic Nick Roddick cites Telluride as one of a handful of festivals that matter to 'the film business' (2013 [2009]: 181). His list also includes Cannes, Sundance, Rotterdam, Berlin, Venice, Toronto, and Busan, all dramatically larger and longer mega-festivals.[2] (Increasingly a marketplace for buying and selling films, Toronto showed 288 films in 2013, whereas Telluride's main slate included just 27 new movies. So the gatekeeper function of Telluride's programming team remains much stronger.) Telluride's position confounds the otherwise clear distinctions that critic and programmer Mark Peranson makes, in *Dekalog 3: On Film Festivals*, between 'business' festivals and 'audience' ones, with business-oriented festivals having significantly higher-budgets as well as marketplaces, press junkets, competitions, premières, corporate sponsorship, large staff, and the like (2009).

Over time, Telluride has become a big-budget event chock-full of visiting filmmakers, premières, sponsorship, and a large staff, but without markets, red carpets, press junkets, or competitions. (The highly curated New York Film Festival occupies a similarly overlapping position as a largely audience-oriented festival, though over time it has welcomed more extensive media coverage, press conferences, and red carpets.) Although the Rocky Mountain gathering continues to offer a select programme with fewer of the trappings of the festival behemoths, it has recently muscled its way into discussions of would-be Oscar contenders, with a strong track record of previewing eventual Best Pictures: *Slumdog Millionaire* (Danny Boyle, UK, 2008), *The King's Speech* (Tom Hooper, UK, 2010), *The Artist* (Michel Hazanavicius, France/Belgium/USA, 2011), *Argo* (Ben Affleck, USA, 2012), and *12 Years a Slave* (Steve McQueen, USA/UK, 2013), all world premières at Telluride, except for *The Artist*, which had its first screening at Cannes. As film scholar Thomas Elsaesser suggests in 'Film Festival Networks: The New Topographies of Cinema in Europe', just as fame at a prestigious festival confers value on a film, the subsequent success of the movie itself further raises the profile of the festival (2005: 101).

2.1 The Abel Gance Open Air Cinema honours the French silent film pioneer and also hearkens back to Telluride's early emphasis on revivals and silent classics, which continues today in muted form. © Jeffrey Ruoff

Telluride 2013, the 40th anniversary year of the festival, provides a good moment to not only take stock of the festival's recent incarnation, but also to chart how it got there from its beginnings. I attended the 2013 festival and — in addition to conversing with other attendees, researching the official Telluride archive at the Margaret Herrick Library at the Academy of Motion Picture Arts and Sciences in Los Angeles, and researching materials from the festival headquarters in Berkeley — was also fortunate to interview afterwards a wide variety of people associated with the festival as well as former attendees. Unless otherwise noted, quotes and paraphrases attributed to these figures come from these interviews.[3]

By juxtaposing the first Telluride film festival in 1974 with its 40th anniversary in 2013, I hope to create a kind of perceptual shock, in which continuities and discontinuities emerge starkly. While many features remain, the contrasts between the first festival and the 40th are suggestive of historical changes in the overall festival landscape, general as well as specific to Telluride. The festival's gradual emergence on the world stage competing for attention with Venice and Toronto could not have been anticipated from its small, but enterprising, origins. Although

2.2 For the opening night dinner in 2013, crowds of regular pass-holders, filmmakers, actors, critics, and exhibitors fill the historic centre of Telluride. © Jeffrey Ruoff

Telluride hardly takes place in a global city, it has nevertheless become a global festival, making it a significant exception to what film scholar Julian Stringer describes in his essay 'Global Cities and the International Film Festival Economy' (2001).

Going from an informal 'mom-and-pop' operation in the 1970s with an initial budget of around $10,000, Telluride has expanded into an international festival with a 2013 budget of more than $3.4 million. Originally, Telluride was programmed more like an archive, with a strong emphasis on revivals and silent classics (figure 2.1). Instead of prizes for new films, the festival has always offered Silver Medallions, which recognise the careers of important film artists. As the decades have passed, the festival has become known as a place where discoveries could be made of both new and old films, mostly American and European, some Asian. Nowadays, revivals, while important, take a back seat to premières. Initially attended in 1974 by some 300 visitors and townspeople, the festival in 2013 welcomed more than 3,500 pass-holders (Horn 2013), and a significantly more upscale demographic, as well as stars and famous directors galore (figure 2.2). Likewise, the number of theatres and staffers has mushroomed over the years.

Surrounded by inviting 12,000-foot mountain peaks, the village has morphed from a rundown mining town to a chic resort with fancy hotels, condos, restaurants, galleries, and boutiques that support a year-round tourism industry. It is an uber-wealth zone now, where the 1 per cent live or own additional homes. The transformation of the town has impacted the character of the festival and vice-versa. Like other festivals as they mature (de Valck 2012: 33–34), Telluride has gradually professionalised, institutionalised, and commercialised, with a considerable expansion in corporate sponsorship and donations. In 2013, the three directors of the festival were co-founder Tom Luddy, programming Telluride for the 40th consecutive year; Gary Meyer, a long-time attendee and affiliate of the festival; and Julie Huntsinger, whose film career began as an assistant to Luddy at American Zoetrope, where she rose to production supervisor for features (Adams 2007). After Bill and Stella Pence retired in 2006, the new team continued to follow long-established traditions, even while accelerating an emphasis on celebrity and high-profile films.

Telluride began in 1974 as an intimate festival of repertory and art house movies for a small audience of film lovers and industry professionals, including speciality exhibitors. Although it does not have a competition with awards, Telluride has, like other prominent festivals such as New York, Cannes, and Venice, become what film scholar David Andrews calls a 'clearinghouse for art cinema' (2013: 179). Over the past decade, as has occurred elsewhere, Telluride has evolved into a launching pad for Oscar campaigns, bending the arc of the festival in a new direction. Telluride's felicitous place in the annual festival calendar has allowed it to step in as the most important North American festival that comes after Cannes. Telluride overlaps with Venice and takes place more than a week before Toronto, and it increasingly competes with both mega-festivals for world or North American premières. As co-founder and former managing director Stella Pence recalls, 'Over the last 10 years or so Telluride has been hot for the next Oscar picture. It's a blessing and a curse. It's the Faustian bargain' (Ruoff 2012b: 152). The initial turn towards award-winning fare featured Anglo-American films such as *The Fog of War* (Errol Morris, USA, 2003), *Brokeback Mountain* (Ang Lee, USA, 2005), *Capote* (Bennett Miller, USA/Canada, 2005), *The Last King of Scotland* (Kevin Macdonald, UK/Germany/USA, 2006), and *Juno* (Jason Reitman, USA, 2007).

As reporter Steve Pond mentions in *The Wrap* in 2013, 'Telluride has established itself as one of the prime places to see contenders for the first time, and it draws enough awards-watchers to create an immediate buzz as effectively as Toronto'. Telluride programmers have developed and sustained close ties with independent distributors, sales agents, studios, and filmmakers that have allowed the festival to screen increasingly high-profile films. Without giving out prizes or having a marketplace for films, Telluride, like NYFF, nevertheless confers on successful movies something which Czach calls 'critical capital' (204: 82). Support from programmers, critics, and other influential audience members often sets the stage for success at other festivals and during theatrical distribution (Elsaesser 2005: 91). Further discussed in specialised journals such as *Film Comment*, *Cineaste*, as well as online sites devoted to motion picture arts, a select few movies shown at Telluride become the most talked about art films of the season. Once a 'little festival' on the periphery, Telluride now occupies a place at what Julian Stringer calls the 'dominant centre' (2001: 138) of the international festival network, despite taking place in a town with a population under 2,500.

A Brief History of the Telluride Film Festival

The 40-year history of Telluride has been marked by gradual but notable shifts, as the annual programme brochures, the Academy archive, and interviews with participants reveal. Like other festivals, Telluride has grown in a variety of ways: the number of films shown, the number of passes sold, the number of venues, the community of attendees, and the size of its staff, volunteer base, and budget. What follows is a concise sketch of the festival's evolution from 1974 in programming, attendees, costs and sponsorship, size, and the remaking of the town, before returning to a longer analysis of the festival's 2013 configuration, which amplifies many features in this historical review.

In its first decade, the festival organisers followed general patterns established in 1974. The schedule usually consisted of just 14 main screenings, which included career tributes. It remained concentrated over a short and intense holiday weekend. As Sony Pictures Classics co-founder and co-president Michael Barker told me, 'Telluride takes place over Labour Day weekend and only people with a sincere and obsessive passion with film give up their holidays to attend a film festival'. If you could get to Colorado, the festival continued to be relatively inexpensive to attend. In 1979, a festival pass cost $75 (Wolf 1979), or $240 in 2013 dollars. For years, the principal venue was the vintage 1914 Sheridan Opera House, which lent a historical dimension to the festival, complemented by the well-preserved nineteenth century red brick buildings downtown. Telluride remained a largely democratic event in which film lovers mingled freely with stars, visiting filmmakers, critics, and art house exhibitors, watching and discussing essentially the same programme.

The original triumvirate of Jim Card, Bill Pence, and Tom Luddy brought different, but complimentary, skills to programming. After 1977, when Card left the festival, Pence and Luddy replaced him with fellow film collector and New York University professor William Everson.

A specialist in silent cinema and American genres, Everson authored numerous books, including *American Silent Film* (1978) and, as early as 1969, had programmed retrospectives for NYFF (Kern et al 2012: 186). With a personal collection of more than 4,000 feature film prints (Grimes 1996), Everson focussed on classics and silent film revivals, until he retired from Telluride in 1987. The co-founders have remained comparatively stable over time, with the Pences working on the festival for 33 years and Luddy still at the helm in 2015.

Telluride's programmers have always welcomed additional presenters. After screening his own films in 1974, Kenneth Anger returned the following year to give the first live presentation of film clips and slides accompanying his book *Hollywood Babylon* (1975). A highlight of the festival, the presentation began at midnight and, per staffer Jim Bedford, Anger showed clips all night long and 'told stories until 8am when about 35 people were still there to go to breakfast with Anger in the morning'. Also during the second festival, Albert Johnson, artistic director of the San Francisco International Film Festival and a major influence on Telluride's tributes, presented an evening of clips from American musicals, concluding with a complete Technicolor print of *Funny Face* (Stanley Donen, USA, 1957). In 1979, Stan Brakhage, by then a regular attendee, presented the restored version of *Que Viva Mexico* (Sergei Eisenstein, Mexico/USA/USSR, 1931–79). The presence of these talented figures enhanced both the live dimension of the festival and its reputation.

In its first decade, Telluride distinguished itself by celebrating the history of classical Hollywood and other repertory traditions. By contrast, the Edinburgh International Film Festival was more polemical in its 1970s programming and retrospectives, promoting a radical reappraisal of Hollywood 'B' movies, as film scholar Matthew Lloyd demonstrates (2011). Unlike many festivals of the era, Telluride staked its original identity around films from the past. In-person tributes in the first decade went to significant historical figures, such as directors Henry King, King Vidor, Hal Roach, Abel Gance, animator Chuck Jones, actors Sterling Hayden and Joel McCrea, editor/director Robert Wise, and cinematographer Karl Strauss. (These were balanced by Silver Medallions given to younger artists such as Jack Nicholson, Werner Herzog, and Robert Altman, establishing a dialogue between an older canon and a newer one.) Tributees typically stayed for the duration of Telluride, taking in additional screenings and participating fully in the festival.

In 1977, a daring programming innovation occurred when the Telluride directors decided to stop announcing their schedule ahead of time. This was more or less unprecedented in the history of film festivals as the programme is typically used to lure audiences. When an invited celebrity had to cancel at the last minute in 1976, the organizers felt embarrassed by press coverage that accented the missing star (Ruoff 2012b: 142). At the time, the festival was not seeking to grow, simply to retain its core audience. Trusting the programmers, regular Telluride pass-holders took the leap of faith; the annual programme has remained a well kept secret ever since. This radical step distinguishes Telluride from virtually all other film festivals and has had numerous implications over the years.

In the late 1970s, film collector, historian, and director Kevin Brownlow made multiple presentations at Telluride. As was the case with Everson, Brownlow's involvement with the festival deepened Telluride's engagement with professional film critics and historians. In 1979, Brownlow's restored 35mm print of Abel Gance's *Napoléon* (*Napoleon*, France, 1927) contributed to one of Telluride's most memorable screenings (Ruoff 2012b: 140; Wagner 2013: 237–8). Still less than half of the 1979 main programme featured new films. In 1980, Tom Luddy left his position at the Pacific Film Archive to join American Zoetrope as a producer and executive, which eventually gave the festival co-founder a producer's perspective on programming.

In 1981, Telluride hosted the first-ever public screening of Louis Malle's *My Dinner with Andre* (USA) with performers Andre Gregory and Wallace Shawn bringing a touch of New York art world sophistication to the little Colorado town. A great success on the art house circuit, the première of *My Dinner with Andre* was a breakthrough for the programmers as well (Ruoff 2012b: 151). In the 1980s, the always heavily curated Telluride eventually began an open submission process, which over the years has contributed comparatively few titles — unlike, for example, at Sundance — as the organisers generally work through tried-and-true associations with other festivals, sales agents, filmmakers, distributors, etc. Despite the ongoing involvement of Stan Brakhage, Telluride's investment in avant-garde cinema gradually waned.

In the 1980s and after, other major festivals such as Cannes, Berlin, Venice, Rotterdam, New York, and Locarno played significant roles in discovering and promoting the emerging cinemas of Asia, Africa, the Middle East, and Latin America. Telluride — more mainstream, Eurocentric (including Central and Eastern European film), and Anglo-American — has shied away from supporting cutting-edge international auteurs such as the Iranian Abbas Kiarostami, Hsiao-hsien Hou from Taiwan, the Chinese Zhangke Jia, and the Hungarian Béla Tarr. Although the festival occasionally featured films from the Philippines, the People's Republic of China, or Tunisia, Telluride has never been in the vanguard of promoting cinemas of developing nations. It has upheld a more restricted canon of the 'best' of art cinema.

In 1987, programmer Bill Everson retired, believing, according to the Pences, that the possibilities for revivals had played out, as archival films became more broadly available through other means of distribution. Pence and Luddy then came up with a novel idea for keeping programming fresh, particularly in terms of retrospectives and classics. Instead of adding a regular member to complete their triumvirate, they would annually invite a different, well-known, guest director. In 1988, they reached out to film scholar Donald Richie, a specialist of Japanese cinema. Soon, Pence and Luddy decided to venture outside of film proper, inviting performance artist and musician Laurie Anderson to guest direct in 1991 and novelist G. Cabrera Infante in 1992. As Pence remembers, 'We thought the guest director should be a person who could bring other arts to Telluride; a musician, a visual artist. We tried to expand the view of what a film lover could be' (Ruoff 2012b: 150). Subsequent guests have included theatre director Peter Sellars, novelists Salman Rushdie and Michael Ondaatje, and musician Caetano Veloso, among others, some of whom have continued as devoted attendees over the years. Many guest directors have greater name recognition, even star power, than the films they introduce, so their presence helps draw viewers to archival screenings and adds cachet to the festival.

Although identified as a cinéphile festival, focussed on the aesthetics of film, Telluride has always had an industry component, and it was attended from the beginning by a number of independent exhibitors of specialised cinema. In 1975, Gary Meyer, Steve Gilula, and Kim Jorgensen founded Landmark Theatres while attending the second festival. That same year, a new Association of Specialized Film Exhibitors came out of Telluride, as an alternative to the more commercial National Association of Theatre Owners. According to Meyer, the loosely knit group, whose members included Theodore Pedas, Larry Jackson, Meyer, and other art house exhibitors, met annually at Telluride for a dozen years, to the consternation of the Pences, who did not want any business conducted at the festival. This kind of exhibitor presence throughout the 1970s and 1980s presaged the later, and more extensive, involvement of industry professionals.

In the late 1980s, as long-time attendee Howie Movshovitz recounts, Bill Pence had the idea of adding a 'Student Symposium' to Telluride to counter declining interest in classic films. Pence knew he could get the symposium funded — director Steven Spielberg provided support in its early years — and he also realised that students could be channelled to more offbeat and obscure screenings, thus creating a built-in audience for revivals, silent films, documentaries, and foreign films. In addition, the younger students would counterbalance the ageing population of Telluride pass-holders. Hosted by Movshovitz, a University of Colorado, Denver, professor and his University of California, Berkeley, colleague and friend Linda Williams, the symposium annually subsidises and welcomes around 50 students, feeding the original cinéphile spirit of the festival.

In terms of sponsorship, there was very little during the festival's first five years, although a handful of benefactors contributed donations. It was principally underwritten by ticket sales, and ran deficits, over $66,000 by 1978 (Wolf 1979) or $235,815 in 2013 dollars. Eventually, the organisers sought to put the festival on more sound financial footing, even preparing a 1979 move to Aspen, Colorado (*Telluride Times* 1979a: 2). According to then festival coordinator Jim Bedford, 'The town of Telluride, the ski area, and the festival met, and ski resort co-owner Ron Allred made a commitment to support the festival so long as the town did, and the town made a commitment to support the festival so long as Allred did'. As the Academy archive indicates, of the 1979 festival's $118,000 budget, $53,000 came from donations, an increase of $35,000 over 1978. From 1979 to the present, mutually beneficial partnerships between the festival, the town, and the ski resort would continue to strengthen, highlighting the much discussed nexus between festivals and tourism (Stringer 2001: 141). Public and corporate funding made it possible to pay more staffers and to run the festival without deficits (Ruoff 2012b: 151). Bill Pence recalls that as another means of expanding its resources, in 1979 the festival introduced more expensive Patron Passes, which granted the holders special privileges. This move represented a step away from the egalitarianism that characterised the initial editions, a trend that would expand over the years.

Frontier Airlines brought additional corporate support in the early 1980s, even receiving front page billing on programme brochures. When Telluride hired a fundraiser in 1985, sponsorship and donations correspondingly increased. Walt Disney Pictures and *The Village Voice* became sponsors, as did, in time, *Premiere Magazine*, as well as increasingly prosperous local realtors. By the 1990s, sponsors included The Discovery Channel, Apple, Miramax Films, and Turner Classic Movies, among many others. In 1998, for its gala 25th anniversary, Telluride received support from the Writers Guild of America, the Directors Guild of America, the Screen Actors Guild, Kodak, and Dolby, demonstrating the festival's growing symbiotic ties to the film industry. Equally important was Telluride's extensive private donor base, which has expanded from year to year. Increased sponsorship went hand-in-hand with the growth of the festival. By 1998, the budget had increased to $1.8 million (Turan

2001: 148) or $2.6 Million in 2013 dollars.

Gradually, the festival expanded its venues, adding a temporary Masons Hall Cinema in 1985. (This began Telluride's now long-standing and exceptional tradition of re-purposing various spaces for the festival and tearing the theatres down afterwards, necessitating large numbers of staff and volunteers.) In tandem, the programme expanded somewhat, and by 1988, the main slate featured 23 films, where it has more or less remained to the present, with gradually increasing numbers of sidebar screenings and special events. Throughout, according to production manager Jim Bedford, Telluride sold out its passes every year, with many people turned away. As Bedford remembers, 'Until 1991, we were only on the radar because of the guests that we attracted here and the reputation that we developed as a laid back festival where everyone walks and stars aren't hassled'. Then, the festival embarked on a major expansion in 1991, adding a 600-seat theatre and doubling its pass-holder base. (A bigger venue also presupposed films that would attract larger audiences than before.) This expansion required more extensive collaboration with the hospitality functions of the town, hotels, restaurants, etc. Telluride was becoming more like other festivals; it was possible to attend and see a different set of movies from other festival goers. As co-founder Stella Pence remembers, 'Somewhere around the 25th year, it was no longer the case that you could count on everybody seeing the same films'.

In the meanwhile, during the 1970s, 1980s, and 1990s, the town of Telluride was booming. By the mid-1970s, housing prices had quadrupled (Lichtenstein 1975). The Idorado Mine closed in 1978, marking the end of an era. That same year, entrepreneur Joseph Zoline sold his ski area to two Colorado natives, owners of the Benchmark Corporation (*Telluride Tales* 2012: 5), who eventually helped turn Telluride into a popular year-round resort, known most of all for its 'white gold' — snow. Other festivals emerged, including Bluegrass, Jazz, Chamber Music, and Mountainfilm (a documentary showcase), all of which broadened the appeal of the town (Duffy 2012: 3). In 1987, the Telluride Airport opened, representing a further revamping of the village as a ski resort and tourist destination. Well-to-do folks started building and purchasing vacation homes, further driving up housing prices in the valley. Telluride had once again become a boom town, the first being during the gold rush of the 1890s. Speaking of the old Victorian houses for sale in the 1970s, festival co-founder Luddy joked, 'If I had bought one or two of them, I'd be a millionaire today'. Whereas there is an established history of European festivals opening in resort and spa towns, Telluride was a festival *before* it was a resort. But just as the festival has branded the town, so the town has branded the festival (Stringer 2001: 140).

2.3 To reach the Chuck Jones' Cinema, pass-holders ride a free gondola from downtown Telluride to the new Mountain Village. © Jeffrey Ruoff

A watershed event in the metamorphosis of the town was the opening of Mountain Village, an exclusive new resort with condos and boutique shops, a gondola ride above the old historic centre. Developed by the Benchmark Corporation, work on Mountain Village began in the mid-1980s, with its first hotel opening in 1992. Since the resort sold upscale condos, the festival audience eventually included more affluent, mainstream filmgoers, eager to see the most popular titles before they were released in regular theatres. The festival itself expanded into the Mountain Village in 1999, with the construction of the 500-seat Chuck Jones' Cinema (figure 2.3). In 2005 and 2006, the 500-seat Palm and 135-seat Le Pierre were added, further expanding the festival experience for the growing numbers of pass-holders. As Bill Pence recalls, 'All of this growth was wanted and, we felt, needed. It made it possible to pay the airfares of the guests' (Ruoff 2012b: 152). As the town grew and became more expensive, the festival got bigger and became more costly both to stage and to attend. By 1998, regular passes cost $500 (Turan 2001: 148), $714 in 2013 dollars. When Stella Pence and Bill Pence retired in 2006, there were more than 2,500 seats in seven indoor spaces, a 700 per cent increase over the audience capacity in 1974, the festival's inaugural year. The new team of Luddy, Meyer, and Huntsinger preserved many of the festival traditions — the secret programme, guest directors,

2.4 In 2013, Telluride feted its 40th anniversary with a gala presentation of new and classic films, supported by high levels of commercial sponsorship and donations. © Jeffrey Ruoff

well-known presenters, in-person tributes to famous figures, premières and revivals, expansion of venues and pass-holders, of sponsorship, of costs and budgets, but added an increasing emphasis on drawing celebrities and introducing high-profile films, particularly in the category of 'sneak previews'.

The 40th Anniversary

In 2013, Telluride celebrated its 40th anniversary with a gala presentation of new and classic films in the now-upscale Rocky Mountain resort (figure 2.4). Befitting this commemoration, the festival harnessed significant star power: big-name actors, directors, literary figures, critics, publicists, distributors, and other notables flocked to the Labour Day weekend jubilee. In all, as the programme brochure notes, Telluride 2013 hosted at least 157 distinguished guests, including Francis Ford Coppola and his granddaughter Gia, premièring her *Palo Alto* (USA, 2013). Usually four days long, the festival was extended an extra day for this historic occasion. For the 3,500 pass-holders and other attendees at Telluride, 2013 was a stormy happening both on-screen as a 'survivalist' theme appeared in works such as *12 Years a Slave*, *All Is Lost* (J.C. Chandor, USA, 2013), *Gravity* (Alfonso Cuarón, USA/UK, 2013), and *Tracks* (John Curran, Australia, 2013), and off-screen, as outdoors the high mountain weather was ever changing.

2.5 Sponsored by CBS Films, a free afternoon concert by the Punch Brothers, a band featured on the soundtrack of *Inside Llewyn Davis*, opened the 2013 festival. © Jeffrey Ruoff

Film festivals, of course, typically offer much more than movies. Telluride 2013 opened with a free afternoon concert by the Punch Brothers, a band featured on the soundtrack of *Inside Llewyn Davis* (Ethan and Joel Coen, USA/UK/France, 2013), which had its North American première at Telluride. CBS Films, distributors of the movie, sponsored the outdoor performance (figure 2.5). Initially sunny, the sky darkened and exploded in a torrential rainstorm, calling a halt to the performance as concert goers sought refuge from the downpour. The mood remained convivial, however, as old friends greeted each other and discussed the programme of the festival ahead, which had just that day been unveiled. Inevitably, the setting of a tiny Western town in Colorado presents a more intimate atmosphere than those of urban festivals such as Toronto, Venice, or Berlin. 'At Telluride, we're all captives', critic and long-time attendee Phillip Lopate remarked, 'while at the New York Film Festival everyone disperses as soon as they hit the sidewalk'.

Like other major international festivals, Telluride draws people from far and wide. Many of the same folks return year after year, either as pass-holders, filmmakers, staffers, or volunteers, forming something of an in-crowd. Following a lightning storm, Radius Films distributor Tom Quinn snapped a photo of old friends Errol Morris and Werner Herzog hugging hello underneath a double rainbow, posted on *Hollywood Elsewhere* (Quinn 2013) shortly before the world première of Morris' *The Unknown Known* (USA, 2013). 'I don't consider Telluride to be a regular festival', Herzog told me. 'You don't have competitions, you don't have media, you don't have a market, and so it's a wonderful family reunion'. A long-time regular since he received a tribute in 1975, the German director comes whether or not he has a new film because 'there are always discoveries at Telluride'. Filmmakers at Telluride actually have time to watch other movies, rather than just promote their own, which provides a welcome change from press-oriented festivals such as Toronto, Cannes, and Berlin. (Herzog recalls once having done 110 interviews at Cannes on behalf of a new film.)

More than other festivals, Telluride is a *conversation*. Standing in line for screenings provides occasions for interaction among filmmakers, critics, and other audience members. Waiting outside the Nugget Theatre, critic, programmer, and filmmaker Mark Cousins summarised for me the special features of the Rocky Mountain event: Telluride is a film festival 'distilled', like 'triple espresso'. A pool of global film and literary talent finds itself in a few square blocks of an out-of-the-way town for a long holiday weekend. Since Telluride now schedules mostly North American and world premières, with their directors present, nervous excitement and anticipation hangs in the air. 'It's an emotional roller coaster, like the peaks and the valleys of the landscape itself', Cousins mused. Telluride also defines itself by what it, unlike most major festivals, has never offered: events staged for the press, prizes, paparazzi, or an organised marketplace. Because the town of Telluride itself is so small, Cousins remarked, 'movie-going is the only game in town, so everyone is totally focussed on it'. Moreover, since the festival principally sells passes, rather than individual tickets, attendees are generally opting for an immersive experience. While large crowds now flock to middlebrow Oscar hopefuls, film lovers like Cousins seek out more rarefied works in the programme, lesser-known foreign movies, documentaries, and revivals of little-seen classics.

Community

Telluride generates noticeable loyalty among its pass-holders, invited guests, staff, and volunteers. Organisers and attendees like to characterise the festival as a community, a feature festivals attempt to create (Elsaesser 2005: 94). Like Herzog and Morris, certain directors typically return year after year — Ken Burns, Jason Reitman, and Alexander Payne — as well as resident curators such as Pierre Rissient, Godfrey Reggio, and Paolo Cherchi Usai. Distributor and producer Michael Barker proudly shared

2.6 Film critic, long-time attendee, and quasi-staffer Leonard Maltin introduces the world première of *Tim's Vermeer* at the Sheridan Opera House at the 2013 festival. © Jeffrey Ruoff

with me that he has attended every Telluride festival since 1981. Critics such as A. O. Scott, Joe Morgenstern, Leonard Maltin, Scott Foundas, John Horn, and David Thomson are frequently found there, and the late Roger Ebert, to whom Morris dedicated *The Unknown Known*, rarely missed it (figure 2.6). Ebert famously said that Telluride was 'like Cannes died and went to heaven' (Loden 2011). In 2013, critic Todd McCarthy, working for *Variety* and now *The Hollywood Reporter*, attended Telluride for the 38th time (Shoff 2013). Telluride has worked systematically to incorporate these prominent figures into the festival. Drawn into its orbit, McCarthy does on-stage interviews with filmmakers, as do Foundas and Maltin, and McCarthy, Foundas, and Barker penned notes for the 2013 programme brochure, thus blurring lines among critics, distributors, and staff.

Pass-holders are often long-term regulars, too, as are audience members at NYFF. Per co-director Gary Meyer, 'Telluride is a festival that is about community, which it has in common with themed festivals like Jewish or gay and lesbian film festivals. The community of people who come back year after year are like old friends, together for a common goal: everyone is ready to discover great new and old films'. Festival badges indicate the number of years a pass-holder has attended, and

2.7 At Telluride, one spends a fair amount of time waiting in line for films, which, at its best, leads to conversations and debates with other festival goers about movies and the programme. © Jeffrey Ruoff

it is not infrequent to meet people who have come to the festival more than 10, 20, or even 30 times. As Herzog says, 'The audience is stable at Telluride. So you see people who have been attending for 20 years and they have seen your last 20 films, so the argument has more depth'. By way of contrast, film critic Robert Koehler characterises Sundance as 'a place where more bad films can be seen under awful viewing conditions than any other festival' (2009: 84). Unlike Cannes, Toronto, or Sundance festival goers, Telluride attendees do not complain much about the festival; on the contrary, most sing its praises — the relative intimacy, the beauty of the mountains, the comparative absence of hype, the accessibility of filmmakers, the cosiness of the old Western town, the quality of the films and projections, the one-of-a kind screenings and events. More folksy than NYFF, consider that when Ken Burns' *Baseball* (USA) premièred at Telluride in 1994, as Student Symposium co-director Linda Williams recalls, the festival organised a ballgame between town residents and festival participants. Herzog played first base for the visiting team.

At Telluride, one spends a fair amount of time waiting in lines for films, often an hour for a feature (figure 2.7). An *Indiewire* critic reported waiting in line 90 minutes to see the first North American screening of the 107-minute *All Is Lost* (Brody 2013). As at a rock concert or other exciting live event, waiting in line fosters anticipation and interaction. While some might prefer to spend more time watching movies, Telluride manages to turn standing in line into an asset. Critic Eugene Hernandez observes, 'In the 10 years that I've been attending the festival, the bonds built while standing in line for a Telluride movie have become lasting friendships' (2013b). One of the downsides of community, as another pass-holder mentioned, is the predilection of programmers to select movies based on long-lasting friendships with filmmakers, rather than individual quality, a kind of allegiance that affects other international festivals.

Programming

Unlike virtually all other film festivals in the world, Telluride keeps its schedule a secret until a day before it begins. (Most influential festivals capitalise on regular press releases that serve up their programmes in advance, building audience interest, prestige, and branding. Cannes offers a relentless stream of announcements in the months leading up to the annual May festival, announcing its jury, its galas, its premières, and so on.) Telluride's secrecy — dating back to Jeanne Moreau's cancellation in year three — serves a number of functions: it gives the programmers flexibility for unexpected changes; it adds an element of surprise; and it levels the playing field for audience members. (As a rule, members of the press do not receive advance screeners for review.) Former co-director Bill Pence notes the versatility of the confidential schedule: 'It provides the audience with a great sense of anticipation. It enables us to have a spot for an important film that arrives at the last minute' (Ruoff 2012b: 142). In practice, this means that visiting pass-holders now shell out upward of $2,500 (for passes, lodging, meals, and travel) based on loyalty, trust, and successful programmes of earlier years. The secrecy also contributes to the mystique of Telluride. Specialised industry outlets now speculate *ahead of time* what movies may or may not make the schedule. As blogger Susan Viebrock wrote before the 2013 programme was revealed, 'Guessing is part of the game we all play' (2013a). For years, the secret programme has allowed Telluride to host world and North American premières without calling them such (this, too, being the opposite of festivals that broadcast the number and importance of their premières or the so-called 'A' list festivals that *must* show premières in juried competitions.)

Telluride screens what its programmers consider to be the 'best' new 23–27 films of the year (a balance of features and documentaries, domestic and foreign), many of which already have or will likely receive

USA theatrical distribution. NYFF offers a similarly small selection of films on its main slate. In this respect, these two American festivals practice an especially granular version of what Elsaesser argues is a paramount function of international festivals, namely to 'categorize, classify, sort and sift the world's annual film-production' (2005: 96). Increasingly, over the last decade, among the movies featured at Telluride are those with Oscar aspirations as well as mainstream studio films. The new works are supplemented by revivals, a dialogue between the new and the old that has always been distinctive of Telluride. As resident silent film curator Paolo Cherchi Usai puts it, 'I'm interested in the relationship between the past and the future of cinema, which is why I like festivals where the past confronts the future, and vice versa. Telluride gives me this. No other festival does to the same degree'. Career achievement tributes, always a mainstay, were given in 2013 to actor-director Robert Redford and Iranian director Mohammad Rasoulof, as well as directors Ethan and Joel Coen and their musical collaborator T-Bone Burnett, with their new movies in tow, *All Is Lost*, *Dast-neveshtehaa nemisoosand* (*Manuscripts Don't Burn*, Iran, 2013), and *Inside Llewyn Davis,* respectively. As these tributes suggest, lifetime awards now go exclusively to active filmmakers/actors who are premièring a movie at Telluride.

Each of the films in the main slate receives a number of scheduled screenings. Intriguingly, when the 2013 Telluride schedule *was* finally released, it still included upward of 40 TBAs ('to be announced' screenings), so that fully a third of the programme remained undisclosed, another strategy undertaken by few other festivals. (As the programme brochures indicate, TBAs began at Telluride in the late 1980s, and have been gradually growing in number, allowing for breathing space in the schedule.) In 2013, these slots allowed room for four sneak previews, de-facto world premières, which included highly anticipated works: *12 Years a Slave*, *Prisoners* (Denis Villeneuve, USA, 2013), *Kaze tachinu* (*The Wind Rises*, Hayao Miyazaki, Japan, 2013), shown just hours after its Venice opening, and *Salinger* (Shane Salerno, USA, 2013).

As well as permitting the sneak previews, the TBA schedule also caters to the tastes and preferences of the public. The programmers take note of well attended screenings and offer repeats to fulfil audience demand. As Bill Pence puts it, 'One of the most exciting things to think about at Telluride, if you look at the programme, is that a clear third of it isn't determined until people get there and start going to movies, letting us know by the seats that they're occupying how that final third is going to play out' (Ruoff 2012b: 146). Telluride gives real programming weight to word of mouth because the movies that gather the most attention get shown repeatedly. In tandem with the growing importance of social media, word of mouth at the small mountain resort still literally means people speaking directly to one another about their favourite screenings, with impressions circulating quickly.

Here is how buzz works at Telluride. *12 Years a Slave* didn't just have a sneak preview; it was shown *five times*, all in TBA slots, which was precisely how the film built tremendous word of mouth. At its first sold-out screening in a 500-seat theatre, director Steve McQueen received a standing ovation together with performers Chiwetel Ejiofor, Michael Fassbender, Lupita Nyong'o, and Brad Pitt (also a producer), all bringing star power to the world première. The full house included Cheryl Boone Isaacs, the first African-American president of the Academy of Motion Picture Arts and Sciences (Feinberg 2013b). So, although Telluride is a tightly curated festival, with the numerous TBAs, the entire third act is, in a sense, programmed by the audience. Furthermore, a range of different size theatres — 140 seats, 150 seats, 185 seats, 230 seats, two with 500 seats, and two more with 650 seats — allows programmers the flexibility to repeat movies in appropriately sized spaces. Keeping pace with strong demand, *12 Years a Slave* consistently played in large venues. Such buzz also helps lesser-known titles. The documentary *Tim's Vermeer* (Raymond Teller, USA, 2013), another world première at Telluride, with three scheduled screenings, had an additional three TBA showings, in a range of different-sized sites. With Penn Jillette, Teller, and subject Tim Jenison on hand, by the end of the Labour Day weekend, co-director Gary Meyer, speaking at an outdoor gathering, referred to *Tim's Vermeer* as 'the sleeper hit of the festival'. So, despite the absence of juries and prizes, the TBA structure fuels Telluride's significant taste making function.

Premières, the Press, and the Awards Season

It is one of the ironies of a mass-produced medium such as film that its initial presentation has become invested with something of the aura of an individual work of art (Ruoff 2012a: 4-5). Trade publications, such as *Variety* and *The Hollywood Reporter*, commit to reviewing every feature at its world première, thus feeding competition among festivals. Furthermore, in the last decade, festivals have become more important because distributors, studios, and sales agents have shifted their attitudes about the prospects for awards, particularly Academy Awards. Since 2006, it has become routine for most Oscar hopefuls to open at one of the major festivals, as long-time Hollywood commentator Anne Thompson notes (2014). Courting the media more than the festival has done previously, co-directors Luddy, Meyer, and Huntsinger held a 'press-orientation meeting' at the opening of Telluride 2013 (Laffly 2013).

Lately, more press has been converging on Telluride as lines blur between traditional outlets, trade publications, and online critics, though the festival continues to require members of the press to purchase passes (unlike most other major festivals). In recent years, as Peter Debruge writes in *Variety*, 'a new kind of journalist started flocking to Telluride. Let's call them the Oscar pundits: a mix of columnists and bloggers obsessed with handicapping the Academy Awards' (2013). Commentators on Telluride 2013 include a long list, some old, others of more recent vintage: the *Daily Mail*, *The Guardian*, the *Washington Post*, *The Wall Street Journal*, the *Los Angeles Times*, *The Denver Post*, *The Huffington Post*, *The Daily Beast*, *Twitch*, *Awards Circuit*, *Deadline Hollywood*, *HitFix*, and *Awards Daily*, among others. The shorthand format of Twitter seems particularly appropriate to the seemingly insatiable obsession with awards. Immediately after the 30 August world première of *12 Years a Slave*, Jeffrey Wells of *Hollywood Elsewhere* tweeted: 'Sad & ghastly as the story is, "12 Years a Slave" is a humanist masterpiece & a slamdunk Best Picture contender right out of the gate' (2013). Even *The New York Times* gets drawn, almost inevitably, into the early awards speculation (Scott 2013). The 'verbal architecture' (2000: 45) that anthropologist Daniel Dayan noted as characteristic of festivals now extends to Telluride in ever more varied formats.

In the past decade, the Academy of Motion Picture Arts and Sciences, which hosts the Oscars, has become increasingly important to Telluride. In 2003, the Academy began supporting the festival financially, and, in 2005, Telluride donated a substantial archive to the Academy, further cementing the relationship (Poland 2005). Beginning in 2005, the Academy in turn committed $50,000 to the festival per year for three years (*Backstage* 2004). Ongoing support continued. For a number of years, the Academy has subsidised the 'Guest Director' programme (McCue 2011). For Telluride's 40th anniversary, drawing on its Telluride archive, the Academy put together an exhibit at the Sheridan Opera House celebrating the festival's history. Significant numbers of Academy members now attend the festival, particularly those based in Los Angeles, a short charter flight away. This mutually beneficial relationship has further solidified Telluride's position at the forefront of early award season speculation.

As well as more Academy members, Telluride has seen increasing participation from studios and distributors, with executives in attendance in 2013 from Warner Bros. (*Gravity* and *Prisoners*), Fox Searchlight (*12 Years a Slave*), and The Weinstein Company (*The Unknown Known*, *Salinger*, *Tracks*), although these relationships date back years. Paramount Pictures brought *Labor Day* (Jason Reitman, USA, 2013) and *Nebraska* (Alexander

Payne, USA, 2013). IFC Films and Roadside Attractions executives were also in town. Sony Pictures Classics co-founders and co-presidents Tom Bernard and Michael Barker have been involved with Telluride for more than three decades. Barker told me that SPC shares its *entire roster of films* beforehand with the Telluride directors, who usually find several pictures that interest them. In 2013, Sony Pictures Classics was well represented at Telluride by *Tim's Vermeer*, *Le passé* (*The Past*, Asghar Farhadi, Iran, 2013), *The Invisible Woman* (Ralph Fiennes, UK, 2013), and *Dabba* (*The Lunchbox*, Ritesh Batra, India/France/Germany/USA, 2013).

As festival co-director Gary Meyer told me, 'Most distributors want to be a part of Telluride, so it works. The specialised distributors want to be part of Telluride, they know that the buzz from Telluride works well with that from Toronto. We might also look at the studio schedule and see if there are films that might be of interest to us'. For several decades, before the rise of social media, other festivals overlooked the notion that a 'preview' at Telluride did not pre-empt a later official première at Venice or Toronto (Ruoff 2012b: 147). At Telluride 2013, French-Canadian director Denis Villeneuve, accompanied by his producers, engaged these semantics in his introduction to the jam-packed opening of *Prisoners*, 'You are the first audience to see this movie. For political reasons I don't understand, this is a sneak preview, but deep in my heart this is the première tonight' (Appelo 2013a). Taking advantage of the secret programme and TBAs, distributors have found sneak previews an important way to launch Oscar campaigns at Telluride, reinforcing the taste making character of the festival.

Whatever kinds of arrangements may have held sway in the past among festivals, in an era of instant online communication, the idea that Telluride can hold a discreet preview in the Rocky Mountains has wavered. The première fetish has caught up with the Colorado festival. As Anne Thompson discusses in *Indiewire*, '2013 marked a watershed year for Telluride, which has long tried to fly under the radar of the fall fests by refusing to announce its line-up in advance and avoiding the usual "World Premiere" nomenclature' (2013). Venice artistic director Alberto Barbera (a guest director at Telluride in 2002 and hence a close associate of the festival) lashed out publicly about Telluride's previews of *The Unknown Known*, *Under the Skin* (Jonathan Glazer, UK, 2013), and *Palo Alto* stealing the Italian festival's thunder (Vivarelli 2013). Likewise, Toronto artistic director Cameron Bailey later stated that films with official premières scheduled at TIFF could no longer be shown beforehand at Telluride (Pond 2014). Regardless of the competition, a significant number of filmmakers at Telluride 2013 were headed to Toronto afterwards. Director Mark Cousins, whose two latest documentaries showed in a sidebar at Telluride 2013, told me he had already lined up 39 press interviews in Toronto before leaving the Rocky Mountains. Sony Pictures Classics managed to screen *Tim's Vermeer* at Telluride, Toronto, and New York, running the gamut of the most influential North American fall festivals, as did Fox Searchlight's *12 Years a Slave*. While festivals may see themselves competing with each other, filmmakers and distributors may find a more congenial festival circuit that increases opportunities for media exposure and, if the films are well received, potential revenues from distribution.

Cinéphile Highlights

Press attention at Telluride 2013 went almost overwhelmingly to Anglo-American pictures with Oscar ambitions, with world premières (especially sneak previews and larger-scale studio movies) garnering extensive reviews and commentary. This media footprint is deceptive as the main slate included 16 foreign films (and eight documentaries), the kinds of less commercial works that have always been a part of Telluride, even if some now get lost in the Oscar chatter, as do the revivals. From a variety of perspectives, Telluride continues to constitute what Elsaesser calls an alternative to the American studio system (2005: 88). Serving an audience of taste makers that travels significant distances and at serious expense, Telluride strives to deliver one-of-a-kind experiences. As Michael Barker recounted, his highpoint of the 2013 festival was a quintessential one-time happening, a slow-motion screening of the Zapruder footage of the Kennedy assassination, played while Don DeLillo read related passages from his 1998 novel *Underworld*.

Everything is done to personalise screenings, so that movies do not stand alone. Each première has a post-film discussion, typically with the director, sometimes also cast members, and usually conducted by a well-known critic. After the North American première of *La vie d'Adèle* (*Blue Is the Warmest Colour*, France/Tunisia/Belgium/Spain, 2013), director Abdellatif Kechiche and actresses Adèle Exarchopoulos and Léa Seydoux answered questions on-stage from Columbia University film professor Annette Insdorf, who has served as a Telluride moderator for decades (figure 2.8). There are public seminars and interviews with film talent, book signings, numerous screenings of short films, and other special events. To satisfy its remaining cinéphiles, Telluride still likes its current fare to be seen in light of cinema's history, though classics now take a 'back seat' to new films, as critic Todd McCarthy summed it up in 'Telluride: Big Premieres Outshine Retrospectives as Festival Throws Itself a Great 40th' (2013).

2.8 After the North American première of *Blue Is the Warmest Colour*, lead actresses Adèle Exarchopoulos (left) and Léa Seydoux (right) pose briefly for a few photographs. © Jeffrey Ruoff

For this anniversary, 13 revival screenings were presented by a variety of dignitaries, including *six* former guest festival directors. Audiences took in Salman Rushdie's presentation of Satyajit Ray's classic *Mahanagar* (India, 1963), while B. Ruby Rich introduced viewers to the revolutionary, feminist *De cierta manera* (*One Way or Another*, Sara Gómez/Julio García Espinosa/Thomas González Pérez/Tomás Gutiérrez Alea, Cuba, 1974). Meanwhile, writers Phillip Lopate, Geoff Dyer, and Michael Ondaatje hosted revivals, as did screenwriter Buck Henry. Reaching further back in film history, Paolo Cherchi Usai presented two silent classics, *He Who Gets Slapped* (Victor Sjöström, USA, 1924), with a new score by the celebrated Alloy Orchestra (a long-time favourite at Telluride) to an enthusiastic audience of 300, and *A Simple Case* (Vsevolod Pudovkin, USSR, 1930), with live piano by Gabriel Thibaudeau to a public of 400. In these more cinéphile-oriented events, perhaps, Telluride best sustains its contribution to what Elsaesser would like to consider film festivals, namely, 'the symbolic agoras of a new democracy' (2005: 103).

The great French documentarist Nicolas Philibert, director of *Être et avoir* (*To Be and To Have*, France, 2002), appeared at Le Pierre, a small space named for his countryman Pierre Rissient, for a sold-out North American première of his documentary *La Maison de la Radio* (France/

Japan, 2013). A love letter to French public radio and the spoken word, *La Maison de la Radio* featured a mosaic of voices and accents. For those who stayed afterwards, the Q&A with Philibert was scintillating. 'The less I know about a subject, the better I feel', the director remarked. 'I prefer spontaneity and chance. I film from ignorance. I don't explain'. But Q&As are not for everyone. Even if they enjoyed the movie and were pleased to see the director there, viewers often scramble out of screenings, likely off to queue for the next film. Cinéphilia is alive at Telluride, but perhaps not as well as in the past. Although co-founder Tom Luddy still hopes to make Telluride 'a little bit of film school' (Hernandez 2013a), critics such as Robert Koehler find more to their cinéphile tastes at the Buenos Aires International Festival of Independent Cinema (BAFICI) or Locarno, which include more adventurous programming, more extensive retrospectives, and more revivals (2013: 72–3).

Staff, Audiences, and Venues

The Telluride Film Festival is a multi-million dollar event with a 2013 staff, including volunteers, that swelled to nearly 900 during the Labour Day weekend (Wright 2013). The staff and volunteers give their time to an experience that Rick Brook, the designated Ringmaster of the Sheridan Opera House in 2013, described to me as 'film camp'. Ninety per cent return each year, according to print traffic manager Chris Robinson. In exchange for room and board, some volunteers come for up to six weeks, while most are in town for only a few weeks. (The volunteer economy plays a significant, and under-appreciated role at film festivals, particularly at the multitude of small festivals run on shoestring budgets that have cropped up around the world.) The ratio of pass-holders to staff/volunteers at Telluride is around four to one, providing a framework for a high level of showmanship (figure 2.9). A viewer from New York City mentioned watching the big-budget *Gravity* in 3D at Telluride because the technical quality of projection was higher than it would be in NYC. Over the years, as it has become more expensive, Telluride has hosted more well-to-do, middle-aged festival goers. As co-founder Stella Pence notes, 'The audience has changed. It's very expensive to go to Telluride. The demographic is quite wealthy. Many are there because they want to be the first ones to see *The King's Speech* [Tom Hooper, UK, 2010]. So we have fewer and fewer die-hard cinéphiles who are making the trek' (Ruoff 2012b: 153). As the attendees have grown older and more affluent, the hundreds of volunteers, many in their twenties and thirties, help keep the festival young and broader-based. As one pass-holder mentioned, 'Without the volunteers, you would just have rich grey-haired people here'. While a less expensive 'Cinéphile Pass' was introduced in

2.9 During the festival, every afternoon in downtown Elks Park, Telluride staff assemble an outdoor theatre for free evening screenings. © Jeffrey Ruoff

2009, it has not countered the extensive costs of travel to, and lodging in, the town.

By 2013, the festival could accommodate more than 3,200 audience members simultaneously in its different theatres. There is a travelling circus quality to the Telluride operation. With financial support from the festival, the town recently converted its outdoor ice hockey rink into an enclosed space that could serve as an indoor venue (Bluetent 2013). In 2013, the festival transformed this pavilion into the new Werner Herzog theatre, with 35mm, DCP, and 3D projection. According to the *Los Angeles Times*, the venue 'required the festival to hire nearly 100 additional staff members' (Wright 2013). A gala revival of the director's *Aguirre, der Zorn Gottes* (*Aguirre, the Wrath of God,* West Germany, 1972) inaugurated the new theatre (figure 2.10). Unlike many festivals, which rent cinemas or own year-round screening facilities, in 2013 Telluride built, and then tore down, six of its nine venues. Its four largest state-of-the-art theatres, which account for 2,250 seats, are built in facilities that normally serve other functions. Local spaces repurposed for the duration of Telluride 2013 include a hockey rink, a Masonic Hall, a middle school gym, a corporate conference centre, a local library, and a high school auditorium. The gathering takes over the small town, turning it into what co-founder Bill Pence calls 'a film festival carnival' (Ruoff 2012b: 148). By

2.10 Constructed in a local hockey rink and inaugurated in 2013, the Werner Herzog Theatre honours the work of former tributee, perennial attendee, and filmmaker Herzog, seen here with the photographer Lena Herzog, his wife. © Jeffrey Ruoff

contrast, because it is located at the established Lincoln Center, NYFF doesn't have to build cinemas, nor does it need to recruit substantial numbers of volunteers to assist in its operations.

During the final stages of the 2013 preparation of the Galaxy Theatre, which included the installation of stadium seating, weeks of work by paid staff and volunteers had transformed a middle school gymnasium into a Georges Méliès inspired site. Later, at screenings of Farhadi's *The Past* and Morris' *The Unknown Known*, both in the presence of their directors, it was difficult to tease out that the setting was once, and would be again, a gymnasium. (Looking up in the darkened auditorium, one could discern folded-up basketball hoops tucked in against the ceiling.) Similarly, Le Pierre, which boasted wall hangings honouring the Cinémathèque Française archive, melted away after the festival, returning to its principal function as a wrestling and climbing gym. Telluride thrives on this kind of 'Penn-and-Teller-like' slight of hand, the showmanship that transfigures an everyday locale into a first-rate theatre (figure 2.11).

2.11 Telluride builds theatres to host its screenings. Local spaces repurposed for the duration of the 2013 festival include a high school auditorium, a Masonic Hall, a middle school gym, a corporate conference centre, and a hockey rink. © Jeffrey Ruoff

Costs and Sponsorship

Staging the Telluride Film Festival cost more than $3.4 million in 2013. Unless you are a staff member, a volunteer, or a guest of the festival, attending Telluride remains a very expensive proposition, as is the case with Cannes, Venice, Locarno, and many other first-tier festivals (Schamus 2012). The Labour Day weekend in Colorado has become the high season for hotels, which cost more than they do during peak ski season, as staffer Chris Robinson pointed out. Nowhere near as hierarchical as Cannes or Venice, Telluride's various passes nevertheless represent a big step away from its once-upon-a-time egalitarianism. In 2013, Telluride's all-purpose Festival Pass went for $780 (figure 2.12). Big-ticket Patron Passes, provided priority entrance, as they have for years, cutting down on the time patrons are required to wait in line. They cost $3,900 each, effectively a substantial donation by the some 380 people who acquired them in 2013. So, notable divisions have emerged among the community of attendees. That said, sales of passes and tickets accounted only for about 38 per cent of the 2013 revenues, with 40 per cent coming from donors and 19 per cent from sponsors (Telluride Film Festival 2014: 66).

2.12 In 2013, Telluride's all-purpose basic Festival Pass cost $780. My attendance at the festival, which included a longer than usual stay to interview staffers and volunteers, in addition to flights from the eastern USA, cost more than $5,000. © Telluride Film Festival

Obviously all this economic activity benefits the town; one local reporter estimated that the festival pumped $1 million into the local economy (Viebrock 2013b).

Unlike in Europe and elsewhere, most American festivals receive little, if any, state or federal support. As at most festivals, sponsorship at Telluride has assumed a much greater role over the years. A donation from entertainment and software company Cinedigm paid for the conversion of the year-round Nugget Theatre to digital projection from 35mm (figure 2.13). The company's COO, Adam Mizel, is a part-time Telluride resident

2.13 A donation from the entertainment and software company Cinedigm paid for the conversion of the year-round 185-seat Nugget Theatre to digital projection from 35mm, a necessity for the festival. © Jeffrey Ruoff

(Sackett 2013). Most aspects of the 2013 festival had a sponsor or donor of one kind or another. As the programme brochure notes, virtually each theatre had a patron — for example, locals Ralph and Ricky Lauren sponsored the Abel Gance Open Air Cinema. The Academy funded the noon outdoor seminars, and Participant Media underwrote a vast Labour Day Picnic. Of greater importance to Telluride than commercial sponsorship is its extremely broad base of individual donors (including foundations), many of them long-term supporters. At least a third of the main slate screenings were backed by donors, including *All Is Lost*, which was 'made possible by a donation from Mort and Amy Friedkin'. A private resident hosted the 2013 'Patrons' Brunch', an occasion underwritten by Land Rover for big-time donors, visiting filmmakers, long-time friends of the festival, press, and patrons. *The Hollywood Reporter*, itself a sponsor, pointed out that one table at the star-studded affair featured actors Robert Redford, Bruce Dern, and Oscar Isaac, together with directors J.C. Chandor, Gia Coppola, and Francis Ford Coppola (Feinberg 2013a). Obviously, there are now multiple communities at Telluride that are, more or less, exclusive.

A local Telluride reporter, who has attended the festival more than 20 times, mentions that 'one of the subtle changes in the festival in recent years has been a growing emphasis on parties and food and socializing events' (Cagin 2013: 3), a further sign of Telluride's growing resemblance to other major festivals. The School of Theatre, Film, and Television at the University of California, Los Angeles, together with *The Hollywood Reporter*, hosted a reception for high-profile guests at the Telluride Gallery of Fine Arts (Appelo 2013b). Ever present, the Academy of Motion Picture Arts and Sciences put on a soirée (Just Jared 2013). At the La Marmotte restaurant, Sony Pictures Classics hosted an annual gathering for members of the press to dine with its directors and stars (Tapley 2013).

Not surprisingly, some old-timers grumble that Telluride is getting too big, selling out to the industry, catering to celebrities, giving in to the pressures of the marketplace, and hyping sneak previews. Waiting in line at the Sheridan for the political thriller *Bethlehem* (Yuval Adler, Israel/Germany/Belgium, 2013), a cinéphile from Massachusetts spoke expansively to me about the festival. A one-time Telluride regular who hadn't been back for 10 years, she became a film buff in college after seeing *Aguirre, the Wrath of God*, so she has always appreciated Herzog's presence. But she finds that patrons disrupt the queues, because one never knows how many may appear at the last minute before the doors open, jumping the long line of ordinary pass-holders. She was disheartened to see studio pictures such as *Gravity* and *Prisoners* screening there, films that would quickly thereafter have commercial theatrical releases. (That said, bigger-budget movies are increasingly found at festivals worldwide, often shortly before their general releases.

The typically highbrow NYFF opened in 2013 with *Captain Phillips* (Paul Greengrass, USA, 2013), offered *The Secret Life of Walter Mitty* (Ben Stiller, USA, 2013) as its gala centrepiece, and *Her* (Spike Jonze, USA, 2013) closed the festival.) Further, the Massachusetts movie lover complained that Telluride has become a 'festival for rich people' and 'elitist'.

Surrounded by an aura of overwhelming patronage, Telluride now finds itself in the resort model of other film festivals such as Locarno, Venice, Cannes, or Karlovy Vary in the Czech Republic. The ongoing transformation of the town has affected the festival as much as anything. One staffer called Telluride 'an extravagant resort'. It has Colorado's most expensive real estate market. Among other wealthy individuals, a number of film and media personalities have owned or now own estates in the area, including comedian Jerry Seinfeld, producers Kathleen Kennedy and Frank Marshall (long-time benefactors of the festival), director Barry

2.14 The vintage Sheridan Opera House, for more than 15 years the Telluride Film Festival's principal venue, no longer lies at the centre of the festival. © Jeffrey Ruoff

Sonnenfeld, actor Tom Cruise (another donor), as well as NBC executive Dick Ebersol and actress Susan Saint James (Gluck 2011).

Compared to other major festivals, because of its brevity, limited number of screenings, and small-town atmosphere, Telluride remains a comparatively intimate, immersive 'film camp' experience that brings domestic and foreign art movies, as well as revivals, to enthusiastic audiences. While NYFF also shows a limited selection of movies, it sprawls out over more than two weeks of principally evening screenings, so daily work routines dilute the heightened festival sense of 'time out of time' (Falassi 1987). Although Telluride now welcomes widespread industry participation, it still isn't set up to function as a market or press junket. Nevertheless, the festival has arrived at a kind of commercial pinnacle, selling out its festival passes to a mainly well-heeled audience, hosting prestigious world and North American premières, playing an early taste making role in the coming awards season, drawing significant corporate sponsorship as well as support from individual donors, and welcoming important directors, stars, authors, exhibitors, distributors, studio executives, Academy members, recreational film fans, and dedicated film lovers, as well as loyal staff and volunteers, to a little town in the Rocky Mountains.

Will Telluride be able to sustain its decades-long dialogue with films of the past? Will the festival be able to have its Oscar cake and eat it too? Under pressure from new media, will the festival be able to sustain its secret programme? Expansion, a feature of virtually all 'business' festivals from Cannes to Berlin to Busan, has gradually reshaped Telluride over its 40-year history. To a degree, Telluride has become a victim of its own success. As one pass-holder laments, 'It's lost some of its soul. Size always does that'. The vintage Sheridan Opera House no longer lies at the centre of the festival (figure 2.14). Thanks to its recent Oscar track record, Telluride basks in unprecedented celebrity. Playing in the festival big leagues, a crucial question going forward, already being whispered in the halls of Telluride, is whether the once principally cinéphile festival will remain in charge of its relations with the film industry, or vice-versa.

Notes

1   Argentinian critic Quintín uses the suggestive term 'festival galaxy' to describe the ways in which various festivals find themselves in orbit around Cannes, the most important one in the system (2009).

2   A form filed with the Internal Revenue Service lists expenses for the 2013 Telluride Film Festival at $3,403,832 (http://pdfs.citizenaudit.org/2014_06_ EO/23-7426302_990_201312.pdf). While exact budgets can be hard to come by, to put the cost of various other festivals in financial perspective, Cannes 2013 disclosed a budget of about $26 million, though it is rumoured to be much higher (http://www.festival-cannes.fr/en/about/factsAndFigures.html), Busan 2013 was more than $11 million (http://bigstory.ap.org/article/busan-film-fest-grows-goodwill-asias-stars), Toronto 2013 came in around $39 million (https://s3.amazonaws.com/media.tiff.net/content/pdf/TIFF2013AnnualReport/index.html).

3   While researching Telluride 2013, I was fortunate to interview the following people in-person, on the phone, and/or by email: co-founders Bill Pence, Stella Pence, and Tom Luddy, Telluride staffers Jim Bedford, Rick Brook, Chris Robinson, and Marc McDonald, Michael Barker of Sony Pictures Classics, resident curator Paolo Cherchi Usai, Mill Valley Film Festival programmer Zoe Elton, filmmakers Mark Cousins and Werner Herzog, critic and novelist Phillip Lopate, Student Symposium leaders Howie Movshovitz and Linda Williams, festival co-director Gary Meyer, former New York Film Festival director Richard Peña, and former Focus Features CEO James Schamus. (While I have not necessarily quoted from all the interviewees, each provided vivid impressions of the festival at different times in its history.) When the interviews took place, all gave permission for their comments to be used. Full citations of these interviews appear in Works

Cited. Of course, at Telluride 2013, I spoke casually with many attendees without knowing their identities, some of whose observations are quoted or paraphrased anonymously.

Chapter 3
Telescoping Telluride

Some hard-core cinéphiles may read this 1974–2013 trajectory of Telluride as a fall from grace, as the initial emphasis on film history, the relationship between the past and the present of cinema, was gradually watered down in favour of premières, high-profile studio movies, and previews of Oscar hopefuls. What film lover wouldn't have wanted to attend the 1977 festival, where in-person tributes went to directors Michael Powell and Agnès Varda as well as art director Ben Carré, with 350 pass-holders ensconced in a town of 1,000, and screenings featured in a vintage opera house? Obviously, it was a rare pleasure for those in attendance. But it would be nostalgic to simply trumpet Telluride in its original form. It was a tiny event, dramatic in the hearts and minds of those who attended, but with little echo beyond the handful of attendees, who took note of the richness of its classic, repertory, and art films.

Festivals, like other institutions, rarely stand still. In recently years, NYFF has expanded its facilities, sidebars, and special events, though it maintains its reputation for showcasing challenging, less-commercial films. Often the only choice seems to be between obsolescence or growth. As with other successful festivals, Telluride evidently chose expansion and, responding to changes in the growing public availability of classic movies, moved increasingly towards highlighting new, often middlebrow, films. Growth went hand in hand with increased corporate sponsorship and private donations. The decline of the festival's initial radical egalitarianism among participants and gradual dispersal of community represents a relative loss of intimacy. The transformation of the town into a wealthy resort serves as a harsh indication of the growing economic stratification of the USA. Unlike festivals that have manifest business orientations, such as Toronto, Venice, Cannes, Rotterdam, Berlin, Sundance, and Busan — which have expanded exponentially in recent years — Telluride remains an audience-friendly festival that attracts a small, but significant, industry dimension.

In the context of a case study, this work on Telluride takes into consideration a wide variety of the axes that Marijke de Valck and Skadi Loist describe in their 'Film Festival Studies: An Overview of a Burgeoning Field' (2009). It highlights Telluride as an institution and considers how its programming practices have conceived of, and defined, film as an art form, discusses the importance of business factors and distribution, and explores the heightened event nature of its exhibition practices.

In addition, this account examines Telluride's singular position in the festival circuit: its emphasis on creating a community atmosphere for its audiences, the overwhelming influence of location and venues on the nature and atmosphere of the festival, changing features of the overall media landscape, and indeed how the above components have shifted over the years, giving the study historical perspective.

What follows telescopes Telluride's distinctive characteristics, which I then analyse at greater length.

1) The unique feature of Telluride in the international film festival landscape remains its secret programme.
2) At its outset, Telluride showed one movie at a time in its main venue, the Sheridan Opera House, so, over the course of the festival, most pass-holders saw and discussed the same films, a situation that persisted for more than 10 years.
3) In the beginning, Telluride staked its identity around revivals and classics, including silent films with live musical accompaniment, in a vintage 1914 opera house, which enhanced appreciation of motion pictures from the past.
4) Over its first decade, Telluride focussed on the rediscovery and straightforward celebration of classical Hollywood cinema, particularly through its tributes, modelled on the San Francisco International Film Festival.
5) From its earliest years, the co-founders have invited others to propose and host special screenings, in many instances of classics and revivals, drawing on the expertise, passion, and name recognition of archivists, historians, critics, writers, filmmakers, and others.
6) Heavily curated, Telluride throws its programming weight behind a comparatively small selection of mostly European and Anglo-American films.
7) Since the 1980s, Telluride's programme has included TBA ('to be announced') slots, up to a third of the schedule, allowing for audience input in programming over the course of the festival and rewarding the most popular movies.
8) Without press conferences, red carpets, paparazzi, a market for sales agents and buyers, or a juried competition, Telluride has nevertheless consistently been able to draw growing numbers of international stars, directors, and industry professionals to a small village in Colorado.
9) The setting of a tiny, historic Western town encourages maximum interaction and conversation among Telluride festival attendees.

10) Compared to all of the other major film festivals, the four-day Telluride remains very short, which makes it more festive, allowing for an especially immersive engagement.

11) Lacking the trappings of most mega-festivals, the comparatively small Telluride has nevertheless gradually found a new niche among major international festivals as an early launching pad for Oscar hopefuls, a shift from its original cinéphile spirit.

1) *The unique feature of Telluride in the international film festival landscape remains its secret programme.* This trademark cuts against the grain of virtually all festivals that lure audiences on the basis of forthcoming movies, visiting dignitaries, etc. Without a programme to publicise in advance, Telluride only prospers through word of mouth about previous editions. In the early years, this gave Telluride programmers free reign to design an exciting compilation of old and new films, with the revivals 'discoveries' as much as were the premières. (In a sense, with the last-minute announcement of the programme, every screening was a 'discovery', particularly before laptops and smartphones.) Pass-holders showed great confidence and loyalty towards the programmers, reinforcing a community of cinéphiles. Perhaps counter-intuitively, comparable to Jean-Paul Sartre's celebrated status as the only person to turn down a Nobel Prize in Literature, Telluride's secret programme has become a mark of its cachet, increasing suspense and intrigue. In later editions, it has allowed for maximum flexibility in coordinating last-minute premières of just-completed movies. No festival has followed Telluride in the unorthodoxy of a secret programme and it is hard to imagine a new or established festival gaining traction this way. At the same time, social media and competition with other festivals increasingly strain Telluride's secret programme, and it may or may not be ultimately sustainable (figure 3.1).

2) *At its outset, Telluride showed one movie at a time in its main venue, the Sheridan Opera House, so, over the course of the festival, most pass-holders saw and discussed the same films, a situation that persisted for more than 10 years.* As such, Telluride facilitated a rich conversation. Clearly, as opposed to festivals that have dozens of different films screening simultaneously, Telluride enhanced its community-building aspect, as pass-holders came together around a common series of screenings, initially 12–14 in the main slate, gradually expanding to around 25. This gave programmers the ability to order screenings in relationship to one another, constructing a grand festival narrative. Eventually, as the venues, sidebars, and number of pass-holders expanded, this distinguishing

3.1 At Telluride 2013, 35mm prints wait in temporary transit to the Film Traffic Office, where the titles are scrupulously kept secret until the day before the festival begins. © Jeffrey Ruoff

feature of Telluride changed, though never rising anywhere near the major festivals that show hundreds of movies. Compared to the mega-festivals, Telluride resembles a summer 'film camp'. This feature of Telluride was established from the outset in the 1970s. Over 40 years, it inevitably evolved as the festival expanded from one venue to 10 venues, from 350 attendees to 3,500 attendees, from one community to multiple communities, but Telluride retained its small town setting and remains just fours days long. Changes at mega-festivals such as Cannes, Venice, Berlin, and Toronto over the same four decades dwarf those that have occurred at Telluride.

3) *In the beginning, Telluride staked its identity around revivals and classics, including silent films with live musical accompaniment, in a vintage 1914 opera house, which enhanced appreciation of motion pictures from the past.* Revivals were the 'tent poles' around which early Telluride was constructed, enhancing a dialogue between the old and the new. Of course, archives such as the British Film Institute, the George Eastman House, and the Cinémathèque Française, among others, were long since in the practice of exhibiting classic films, as were festivals such as New York, San Francisco, and Locarno. In promoting silent cinema

screenings as major events, Telluride played an important role in a broad re-evaluation of early cinema, which occurred simultaneously across the field of film studies and eventually led to festivals consecrated entirely to archival cinema (Marlow-Mann 2013). As Telluride moved towards premières, new festivals emerged — for example, the Pordenone Silent Film Festival in Italy (1982) and Il Cinema Ritrovato in Bologna (1986) — that concentrate exclusively on film restoration, silent, and classic movies.

4) *Over its first decade, Telluride focussed on the rediscovery and straightforward celebration of classical Hollywood cinema, particularly through its tributes, modelled on the San Francisco International Film Festival.* The moment was ripe for bringing in guests whose careers literally spanned decades abroad as well as in Hollywood, in both silent and sound film. Unlike Edinburgh in the late 1960s and early 1970s, however, Telluride for the most part focussed attention on important figures from the past in a non-critical atmosphere of film appreciation.

5) *From its earliest years, the co-founders have invited others to propose and host special screenings, in many instances of classics and revivals, drawing on the expertise, passion, and name recognition of archivists, historians, critics, writers, filmmakers, and others.* From its beginnings, Telluride drew on a special synergy among its four co-founders and three programmers, each of whom brought different emphases, backgrounds, and skills to their tasks. At the highest levels of its organisation, Telluride has always been collaborative and collective. In this spirit, the festival established a revolving stable of returning figures — such as filmmakers Chuck Jones and Ken Burns as well as critics Roger Ebert and Todd McCarthy — who joined the 'Telluride family', writing program notes, hosting screenings, conducting on-stage interviews, and other special events. In 1988, co-founders Bill Pence and Tom Luddy replaced retiring silent film programmer Bill Everson with annual guest curators, not only filmmakers but other artists outside of cinema proper — renowned musicians, theatre directors, and novelists who have lent fresh ideas, especially for revivals, and, by their presence, bring additional prestige to the festival. Despite the recent Oscar chatter, which dominates the media response to the festival, Telluride continues to offer archival screenings for those eager to see older motion pictures well presented in theatrical settings.

6) *Heavily curated, Telluride throws its programming weight behind a comparatively small selection of mostly European and Anglo-American films.* In the current festival galaxy, despite substantive differences highlighted in this account, of the major festivals, Telluride most resembles New

York. (Beginning in the late 1980s, however, NYFF became much more adventurous and international in its programming.) Telluride built its identity around a certain conception of cinéphilia, the love of classic, repertory, and art cinema — its own kind of theme-based approach to community. This represents programming as a form of criticism, since it nominates a limited number of films as the most significant of the season, putting these at the forefront of critical discourse in specialised magazines, such as the Lincoln Center's own *Film Comment*. NYFF and Telluride remain the most highly curated of major festivals, giving them corresponding influence for the prospects for theatrical distribution of new art films and eventual non-theatrical circulation of works that appeal to smaller audiences.

7) *Since the 1980s, Telluride's programme has included TBA ('to be announced') slots, up to a third of the schedule, allowing for audience input in programming over the course of the festival and rewarding the most popular movies.* In this way, successful films receive extra screenings, building buzz and word of mouth, with attention flowing to popular films, rather than the most aesthetically challenging works. (Clearly, distributors see advantages to having movies shown numerous times, not necessarily allowed at other festivals.) Even after announced, Telluride's secret programme has gaps that promise surprises and opportunities. This structure leaves room for 'sneak previews' of new films, increasingly filled by Oscar hopefuls whose distributors find Telluride an ideal platform for rolling out their wares. While other festivals now offer 'sneak previews' as a way around competition for official premières, few have adopted the flexible TBA setup.

8) *Without press conferences, red carpets, paparazzi, a market for sales agents and buyers, or a juried competition, Telluride has nevertheless consistently been able to draw growing numbers of international stars, directors, and industry professionals to a small village in Colorado.* Jim Card's perspective — that 'the success of any film festival depends not on the movies that are shown, but on the guest celebrities that are lured to attend' — has proven prophetic for Telluride. The festival has managed to bring in an impressive slate of guests thanks to its programmers' widespread connections and its well-staged tributes. (A mainstay of Telluride, such tributes have now become commonplace at festivals throughout the world.) From the first year, Telluride set itself apart by fostering a radical egalitarianism among ordinary pass-holders, critics, exhibitors, and distinguished guests, freeing stars to circulate uninhibited. For decades, visiting filmmakers socialised with other attendees in an intimate low-key atmosphere. Although it has grown substantially and now contains

multiple communities, still today Telluride remains a pleasure for filmmakers who enjoy the opportunity to see movies — old and new — rather than simply do publicity for their own projects. And regular pass-holders enjoy the thrill of catching glimpses of stars and famous directors as well as watching and discussing movies.

9) *The setting of a tiny, historic Western town encourages maximum interaction and conversation among Telluride festival attendees.* Co-founder Bill Pence grasped this feature from the beginning, seeing that for all intents and purposes, during its Labour Day weekend run, the festival would be the only game in town. In its early years and to a degree still today, Telluride's relative isolation has drawn a particular kind of pass-holder, often devoted cinéphiles or others with professional interests in repertory and art cinema. (Subsequent gatherings, such as the Midnight Sun Film Festival, started in 1986 in Sodanklya, Finland, have cultivated this sort of atmosphere in even more remote settings.) Increasingly, with the transformation of Telluride into an international resort, audiences have become more well-to-do and inclined to seek out the highest-profile films, shortly before their commercial releases in theatres. Similarly, as the size of the festival has increased exponentially, while festival goers may still find themselves in line with Werner Herzog, it is unlikely now for regular pass-holders to share beers with Francis Ford Coppola, as occurred at Telluride 1974.

10) *Compared to all the other major film festivals, the four-day Telluride remains very short, which makes it more festive, allowing for an especially immersive engagement.* Cannes, Venice, Berlin, Toronto, Sundance, Rotterdam, New York, and Busan all last more than 10 days. Most attendees at Telluride purchase passes, rather than tickets, opting for a package experience. As far as Telluride goes, it is better to stage maximum excitement over a short period and then send everyone home. In addition to parties, attendees focus on the films themselves as well as opportunities to converse about them with other participants.

11) *Lacking the trappings of most mega-festivals, the comparatively small Telluride has nevertheless gradually found a new niche among major international festivals as an early launching pad for Oscar hopefuls, shifting from its original cinéphile spirit.* Aside from the co-founders' ability in 1974 to draw major stars, art house exhibitors, and critics to a festival with no track record, in an obscure village in the Rocky Mountains, nothing in the beginning presaged Telluride's current status and worldwide prestige. For many years, like New York, Telluride steered clear of the première fixation. Telluride's annual brochures have never listed whether or not

a given film represents a USA, North American, or world première. Over time, as newer movies squeezed revivals out of the main slate, the co-founders recognised that an unannounced programme would have to deliver at least North American premières to its cosmopolitan pass-holders. In part because of its place in the annual festival calendar, Telluride managed to thrust itself to the forefront of a peer group of much wealthier behemoths, especially Venice and Toronto. Telluride has done this through close relationships with independent distributors and mini-major studios, redefining its taste-making functions. In the 1980s and 1990s, the small scale of Telluride allowed distributors to 'test the waters' of audience response without the glare of publicity inherent at other major festivals. Telluride has also cultivated a mutually beneficial relationship with the Academy of Motion Picture Arts and Sciences, donating its archive to the Academy in 2005. Widespread participation by Academy members, as well as a plethora of online critics, has now raised Telluride's profile — for better and for worse — as the bellwether of the coming award season, with a track record of premièring Oscar-winning films.

Indeed, in 2014, extending its Hollywood prestige streak, Telluride hosted the North American première of eventual Oscar Best Picture winner *Birdman or (The Unexpected Virtue of Ignorance)* (Alejandro González Iñárritu, USA), just days after its world première in Venice. Meanwhile, other festivals — the TCM Classic Film Festival in Los Angeles (since 2010), Locarno in Switzerland, Midnight Sun in Finland, La Rochelle International Film Festival in France (since 1973), BAFICI in Buenos Aires, and the Jeonju International Film Festival in South Korea (since 2000) — have resisted the lure of (or have not been given the opportunity of hosting) Oscar launches, and now carry on the pure cinéphile spirit that originally animated Telluride. The initial egalitarian atmosphere of Telluride, radical for its time, gradually eroded over decades as the town became more chic and the festival more expensive to attend. Lately, other cinéphile festivals — Midnight Sun, Roger Ebert, Traverse City — have succeeded in sustaining this egalitarian ambience. Nevertheless, in contrast to attendees at mega-festivals such as Venice, Toronto, or Cannes, ordinary Telluride pass-holders may still have a festival experience comparable to those of studio executives, Academy members, and art house distributors.

Chapter 4
Programming the Old and the New: Bill and Stella Pence on the Telluride Film Festival[1]

In 1983, the Pences relocated from Colorado to New Hampshire, when Bill was appointed Director of Film at the Hopkins Center for the Arts at Dartmouth College in Hanover, NH. He remains at that post in 2015, programming year-round film series. Stella is a trustee of the Robert Flaherty Film Seminar, and both are advisers to the Chuck Jones Centre for Creativity. They have also consulted with Turner Classic Movies in the creation and programming of its TCM Classic Film Festival, launched in Hollywood in April 2010. I met Bill in 2001, when I came to teach at Dartmouth College, and I have enjoyed many fruitful interactions with him. I eventually had the pleasure of meeting Stella as well. This chapter is based on interviews I did with Bill and Stella on 13 and 15 July 2011, in Wilson Hall at Dartmouth. After Martha Howard transcribed our discussions, I edited the transcript, which was checked for accuracy by the Pences.

Origins

Jeffrey Ruoff: *How did the Telluride film festival start?*

Bill Pence: Well, that first year, 1974, none of us knew anything. We expected this to be a one-time thing. The idea for the festival came from James Card, the film curator at George Eastman House. He was one of the three most influential founders of the international film preservation and archive movement, with Henri Langlois of the Cinémathèque Française in Paris and Iris Barry of the Museum of Modern Art in New York. Card had a romance with the old West: he imagined himself being in one of those old theatres in the mining towns where Lily Langtry performed, like in *The Westerner* [William Wyler, USA, 1940] with Walter Brennan. Jim was a fellow film collector, and he came to visit Stella and me in the early 1970s, when we ran a chain of movie theatres in the Rocky Mountains. He brought some film prints which played in our opera house in Aspen, Colorado, and the next night in our opera house in Telluride. The programme included two silent films, *Lonesome* [Pál Fejös, USA, 1928] and a Japanese film, *A Page of Madness* [*Kurutta ippēji*, Teinosuke Kinugasa, 1926]. In Aspen, the theatre was between 50 and 100 per cent full. In Telluride, the place was jammed; all 232 seats. Of course, there was nothing else to *do* in Telluride.

Stella Pence: We had a captive audience of disaffected hippies, alternative types; people who had moved from the cities to eke out their lives in a hard scrabble community. Most of them painfully well educated. The garbage man probably had three PhDs. Telluride was a town in transition, just right for a film festival. The ski area hadn't been built. Lots of the young people were there.

BP: At the time, I was one of the partners of Janus Films, and Stella and I ran the theatrical division from Colorado. As a result, we knew film exhibitors in art theatres across the country. We presented Janus Film Festivals. Traditionally, they were nine-week festivals: a week of Bergman, a week of Fritz Lang, a week of Kurosawa, a week of Truffaut. So we already knew by phone the best theatre owner in Atlanta, and Bob Laemmle in L.A., and Mel Novikoff in San Francisco. When we decided to do a festival in Telluride, Stella and I would say, 'Gee, we're having a party, this is going to be fun, you know? Francis Coppola, Leni Riefenstahl, and Gloria Swanson are going to be there'. And luckily, a lot of these exhibitors came. I think this planted the seeds that Telluride, from the beginning, was a festival for cinéphiles who cared about and loved the movies.

SP: The exhibitors' outreach into their own communities helped us. There were a lot of people from Denver. Do you remember that first year we ran that bus from Denver?

BP: Yes, exactly. We offered a deal for that first festival: you could get lodging, a full pass for Telluride, and your transportation to and from Denver — $50 a person. *And* you got to meet Coppola and Swanson. We were worried it was too high-priced.

SP: One of the things that's interesting to me about Telluride is that we never started it with high ideals. We were not interested in increasing tourism. We certainly had no great desire to spread the word about how fabulous film was. We mostly wanted to have a big party. James Card came and said, 'Wow, this could be really fun'. He brought us Leni Riefenstahl.

BP: Card also brought Tom Luddy, director of the Pacific Film Archive at the University of California-Berkeley. Tom is probably world cinema's best matchmaker. His phone directory of movie people is infamous.

SP: We thought it would be a one-time, cool event. But it just kept going, took on a life of its own.

BP: Card was a *roué*, a man who had an affair with Louise Brooks. Tom and I loved the balance of the threesome. In the first couple of years, Card was silent film, classic film; Luddy was the future of film, what's happening now; and I was sort of the entrepreneur in the middle, balancing both sides.

JR: *What festivals had you attended before starting Telluride?*

BP: A now-defunct film festival in Aspen, the San Francisco International Film Festival a number of times, Filmex in Los Angeles a number of times, Venice, Cannes, New York, the Flaherty.

SP: The Cork Film Festival in Ireland. Tom has been to a lot more of the exotic ones.

BP: For us, the key ones were San Francisco, which so influenced our tributes, and Filmex, where we learned how eclectic and exciting a festival can be and how much showmanship is involved. San Francisco was the pioneer of great tributes. Unfortunately, they would take all day. I mean, for example, a Howard Hawks tribute would come after seeing eight full features. *A Girl in Every Port* [USA, 1928], *Rio Bravo* [USA, 1959], *Hatari!* [USA, 1962], and *The Big Sleep* [USA, 1946], or whatever. You'd have to sit there for hours. But how wonderful it was to be there with John Ford, Howard Hawks, and David Lean. And, if you talk about a sense of family, nobody does that better than Cork, where everybody sees a film together, then goes to the festival club for drinks. I also liked the Flaherty seminar ideal of a family, with civilised discourse, in a remote, quiet place.

JR: *And perhaps the excitement of Cannes?*

SP: I don't think Cannes is exciting, I think it's terrifying, frenetic beyond belief. On the weekend, you literally can't walk down the Croisette, it's so crowded. And there are police cars everywhere, things are roped off, it's a miserable place to be. Unless you're doing business and you have to be there. Or unless you're in a suite in the Carlton Hotel with more money than God.

BP: In the 30-plus years that we have been going to Cannes, I don't know the total number of celebrity actors and directors we have seen, but not many. Truffaut once gave you a rose, Stella, in an elevator. But we have seen fewer in number over the course of 30 years than an off-the-street, regular guy would experience at Telluride. Because the talent are all kept with their entourages away from people at Cannes. One of the big, magic things about Telluride is that you're bumping into these people all the time.

SP: I think the magical thing about Cannes is the red carpet. By nine in the morning the barriers are in place and people are lining up.

BP: But those aren't the film lovers, those are the French people.

SP: And there's lots of screaming and flashbulbs going off.

Programming

JR: *The mix of old and new films is really one of the novel, defining features of Telluride. What was exciting about this mix?*

BP: There were very few festivals in this country in the 1970s, and the big ones were pretty much all about new films. We began with Jim Card and Tom Luddy, two archivists. The first year, 1974, a lot of the festival was in Card's hands. And his shtick was the classic cinema, older cinema, German films.

SP: Bill was the sole showman. And all his life he's been in love with older films, so Telluride began with people who were enamoured with classic films, as opposed to being star-struck by new movies. We started from a position of zero strength, and a lot of what we could get were older films that we admired. It changed a lot as the festival grew and became bigger and more complicated, as the town grew and became more expensive, less funky.

BP: Less edgy.

SP: More commercial, more high-end. The festival became more powerful, and we could get more new films to go with the old, good films.

BP: In terms of programming, initially Telluride was much more in the direction of the George Eastman House kind of programming — rare treasures and undiscovered masterpieces, King Vidor, Gloria Swanson, Henry King — than it was contemporary filmmakers. That took a long time to change: the balancing act between new films, for example, which had no priority in the beginning, with the focus on retrospectives, rediscoveries, and restorations. Both have been an important part of Telluride. Today [2011] I think the balance is 60/40: 60 per cent new films, 40 per cent revivals.

JR: *Telluride really participated in the rediscovery of silent and classic films, didn't it?*

BP: When Jim Card left, we went to Bill Everson, another classic cinema guy, for the same reason. Everson was a wonderful man — easy collaborator, delightful to work with. He shared classic films at the festival for over a decade.

SP: Bill Everson had a huge following at Telluride. His films were always shown in the community centre because they were on 16mm, from his own collection. He wore a leather cowboy hat, an Aussie hat, and a suit and tie. He was the only person in Telluride who ever wore a suit and tie. He'd go down the street with his 16mm film reels under his arms. He was much loved in Telluride.

BP: If you were to ask me what the watershed event for Telluride was, I would say the revival of *Napoléon* [*Napoleon*, Abel Gance, France, 1927] in 1979. That screening changed the attitude towards film preservation worldwide, of film archiving and silent film. Francis Coppola had his father write a score that travelled internationally to the world's biggest arenas and palaces, to full houses, starting in 1980 at the Radio City Music Hall in New York. That really marked us.

SP: It used to be easy to fill the house with silent films or lost foreign films, difficult films. It's much harder now. The audience has changed substantially at Telluride and the accessibility of films is everywhere. I mean, you press a button on your computer and you can get virtually anything that you want to see. Consequently, the desire to programme those difficult kinds of things is waning a little bit.

JR: *What were you looking for with the tributes in the early years and afterwards? What were the ones that most pleased you?*

BP: First of all, the tributes really identify and stamp what Telluride's all about: the art of film, the appreciation of film. When James Card came, and he wanted to give tributes to Swanson, Riefenstahl, and Coppola simultaneously, it just seemed like a perfect way to do it. Riefenstahl's appearance generated a lot of controversy and got us on the map immediately. Now, tributes are everywhere. But when we started

73

Telluride, some of these greats were alive — what would you have given to talk to Jeanne Moreau, Lillian Gish, Hal Roach, Fritz Lang, John Ford or John Wayne?

SP: The tone for that was set the first year. Coppola represented the new and current, Swanson was the classic Hollywood, and Riefenstahl was the one you hadn't heard about.

BP: In terms of tributes, the ones that I think are the most perfect are the ones that are rare. In the early years, I think it would have been Chuck Jones. He would have been pretty much forgotten by most people in 1976. Michael Powell. I asked Powell years later what Telluride did for him, and he said, 'There was life before Telluride, but life after was much different. I was looked upon as a film director once again'. It was always wonderful to spring a surprise on the audience. 'Where in the hell did they come up with that?' One of the best tribute ideas came from casting director Fred Roos, who suggested a tribute to the American character actor, to the profession. There they were at Telluride 1981: John Carradine, Elisha Cook, Margaret Hamilton, Woody Strode. It was a tribute to that profession, and so to have those faces all within a three-block area in Telluride was really extraordinary. After that, one of my favourite tributes was Joel McCrea, who'd always been an elusive figure. Never liked to mix with the public. We found him at his ranch, somewhere between Los Angeles and San Francisco. The process of getting him to Telluride was like a dance. I'd say two of the defining tributes were Abel Gance and Andrei Tarkovsky, which I think was probably Telluride at its best.

JR: *How did you manage to bring Tarkovsky in 1984?*

BP: We were persistent. It took years. Finally, it became possible to bring Tarkovsky after *Nostalghia* [*Nostalgia*, Italy/USSR, 1983]; he had a visa that would permit him to come to the USA. It was really a very brave thing for him to come. He put his freedom on the line. Then, at a panel for the public, on Main Street — this was not for the press — came the famous debate between Tarkovsky and Richard Widmark. The art versus commerce debate.

SP: Yes, what was the origin of art? Was art born in sorrow and sin, à la Tarkovsky, or was film for fun, à la Widmark? It was wonderful.

BP: Over the years, tributes became less important to the festival itself. They were very important to Tom and me because they were promises to the pass-holders that, although they didn't know the programme, they were for sure going to have three major tributes.

SP: In the early years, Tom started a tradition in which he would fly to Las Vegas, about a week before the festival started, and pick up a bunch of filmmakers, often Eastern European filmmakers. Tarkovsky was on one of those journeys. Tom would load up in a van and drive everyone through Las Vegas, through Monument Valley, up through the American West to Telluride. As you can imagine, they were dumbstruck.

JR: *Unlike most festivals, Telluride doesn't announce its programme in advance. How did this come about?*

BP: We announced our programme ahead of time only for the first three years. The thing that precipitated the change was in the third year. Jeanne Moreau was invited as a tribute guest. She accepted. Then, the week of the festival, she had to go into oral surgery and couldn't make it. We felt we had egg on our face. As people came into town for the festival, the headline on the *Telluride Times* newspaper read, 'Moreau cancels'. That was the final straw. I said, 'Tom, we are *never* going to announce our programme again!' It has paid enormous dividends. It remains almost unique to Telluride. Not announcing creates a certain flexibility when hot films are available at the last minute, or people cancel whom we thought we had on board. It's also part of the egalitarianism since no one has any advance information.

SP: As a result, we're very tough on a new film being a North American première. It's a pact with our audience. We don't tell them what's coming, but they can rest assured they won't have seen what's on the slate before.

BP: I think part of the mystique of the Telluride Film Festival is *anything* could happen. We can fill in a spot that's been cancelled, like five days before. It provides the audience with a great sense of anticipation. It enables us to have a spot for an important film that arrives at the last minute. Often some of the hottest films — *Brokeback Mountain* [Ang Lee, USA, 2005] or *Slumdog Millionaire* [Danny Boyle and Loveleen Tandan, UK, 2008] — aren't even finished until the very, very last moment.

JR: *What has been Telluride's relationship with the press?*

BP: Difficult, although we have received good press over the years.

SP: For starters, there's no such thing as a press pass. Some festivals in the past even had paid press junkets. At Telluride, the press was required to buy a pass just like everybody else. Although we've always had a respectable amount of press, it's never been a love fest. There are no special arrangements made for the press, there are no press rooms.

BP: They're not guaranteed an interview. We certainly don't do screeners so the press can see things in advance. One result was, when Clint Eastwood came, or Helena Bonham-Carter, they didn't feel they had interview obligations. They could let their hair down and enjoy themselves like other pass-holders.

SP: I think that we didn't want the festival ever to be about hype. And don't forget we thought it was only going to be one year. We've always felt that it was better to under-promise and over-deliver. Also, we never wanted it to be about the press; we didn't want the press to overwhelm the film. We were fearsome about entourages. Telluride was not about your publicist's fourth secretary from the left. We wanted to try to keep it as pure as possible, keep it about the films. We were significantly unpleasant to producers for years. After the audience, the people who were important were first the directors and the actors. Also, we never wanted it to be a festival for rich people. Unfortunately, it has turned out that way because of the economics of the town.

JR: *For whom is Telluride programmed and designed?*

BP: The audience. The pass-holder. We've always felt that way from the very start. At the top of our mission statement, in fact, it *says* that the pass-holder is king. At festivals I attended before we undertook Telluride, I always noticed the difference in the way that audiences and press and filmmakers were treated. For instance, I remember a screening at the old film festival in Aspen, in the 1960s. Show time was 8:00pm. The theatre was full, except for the best seats in the house. And it wasn't until 8:25pm that this entourage of festival sponsors, rich people in Aspen, and a couple of the directors, came and sat down in those prime seats, so that 'we the people' could ...

SP: ... admire them as they came in.

BP: That made an impression on us. Also, every time I attend Cannes, which is a festival for the press, I note that everyone else is a second-class citizen. At Telluride, we try to treat everyone equally, to create an egalitarian film festival experience.

JR: *How is the Telluride pass system different from that at Venice, or at Cannes?*

SP: Oh, completely! I mean, at Cannes, there are multiple hierarchies. There's the press, then there's probably filmmakers, distributors, then there's the dweebs on the street. But even within the press, there are seven or eight categories, and if you have the lowest press pass, you are untouchable. You can't get in. We actually worked our way up through various string-pullings, tantrums and fits, to the second-highest pass, which was pink. And even then, there were times when we did not get in at all. It's very frustrating when you're there on business. But it has to have been a nightmare for the people who paid for a pass to see something, and never got in.

JR: *I would imagine that the system at Sundance is similar.*

BP: Their priority is for press, and for filmmakers.

SP: I think you diverged from Tom in this. His concern was always the filmmakers: would they be happy, would they be comfortable, would they mind if they stood in line. We always felt that the pass-holder was more important and that guided everything. In the years we were at Telluride, the only filmmakers who received the best passes, which would enable them to get into the theatre first, were tributees. And people who were infirm. So, it was a difference in philosophy.

BP: And it has worked well. While waiting in line, pass-holders at Telluride inevitably run into filmmakers. You'd never, at Cannes, for example, be able to stop at a concession stand with Roger Ebert, or be in line with Jodie Foster, or something like that. And it just happens all the time at Telluride.

SP: But it's interesting that you asked for whom we programmed the festival. I always had the sense that we programmed the festival for ourselves. It was what Bill and Tom loved, with me kibitzing somewhere in the background. But what was important was that we were proud of the films that we played. We programmed for us under the assumption that either you liked it, you came, and kept coming, or that you chose somebody else's taste and went to another festival. The pass-holder has to trust in us. We promise that we're not going to pander to your tastes. We'll feed you the peas, the coinage of the day, because we think you ought to know about this, and we won't let you down. In his opening remarks at Telluride, Bill always said, 'Don't go see the things that you know all about. Don't go to the things that are familiar to you. Go and see the things that you've never heard anything about, and open your eyes to those things'. People absolutely did that. Those are the great discoveries that you wouldn't get at Sundance, or Toronto.

JR: *To programme Telluride, how did you learn about films that you might want to show?*

BP: The only festival that Stella and I traditionally went to was Cannes. Tom went to many. We relied on 1) what Tom got wind of; 2) Cannes, which is really the gathering place for most films; 3) film distributors calling us; and 4) by our being aware of what films were coming up from important directors, and from studios that we dealt with all the time, like Miramax and Sony Classic; and, finally, 5) an open submission process that brought some pleasant surprises like *The Civil War* [Ken Burns, USA, 1990]. Tom prepared a list of films that we should be tracking all over the world: Japan, India, and so forth. But most of what had been seen in Europe and not in the US came from Cannes. If we found a film we were interested in, we would contact the film's producer — 'Would you like to show your film at Telluride?'

SP: The only time it was difficult was for an obscure foreign film, if there was a pending distribution deal. Then that was a fine line to walk. They had to be sure that the distribution company would be happy if it played in Telluride. I think for American films, it's a little trickier.

BP: It's how it fits into marketing. Most of the high-profile films that play at Telluride have distributors attached. Sometimes, you'd start as far back as the director, then go to the producer, and then to the distribution company; it depends on how far the film has progressed. That was the way with *Lost in Translation* [Sofia Coppola, USA/Japan, 2003]. We went to Sofia Coppola first and worked our way up. It helped that we had been film distributors. We have long-term relationships with distributors and also with sales agents, like Wild Bunch, MK2, Fortissimo.

JR: *Once you have the films, what is the process of deciding when, and where, to show them at the festival?*

BP: With seven theatres, you have to make sure that every new film, for example, plays four times, and you don't want to butt up the only screening of a very specific retrospective, a revival, with another of the same type. You want to give people who love movies the opportunity to see all of the films. I really start thinking about the retrospective choices even before Cannes. It's called slotting. I enjoy the mathematical thing — who would be exiting theatres at a given time. We also wanted to give breathing room. For example, the best possible year was when the theatres would rest for two hours at noon, and people would take time out for lunch, attend the seminar. One theatre now has a noon show, for those people who do not eat lunch and insist on cinema 24 hours a day.

JR: *How do you go about putting the right film in the right-sized theatre?*

BP: I could pretty much tell what belonged where. There were a couple of instances that took us by surprise; for example, *Roger and Me* [Michael Moore, USA, 1989]. The world première was in our smallest theatre, 151 seats, and the lines stretched around the block. It ended up with eight unscheduled screenings, a total of 11. Until they open you really don't know what films, what programmes are going to catch on. TBAs, those 'to be announced' shows, are very much a part of the festival. One of the most exciting things to think about at Telluride, if you look at the programme, is that a clear third of it isn't determined until people get there and start going to movies, letting us know by the seats that they're occupying how that final third is going to play out. This means that the participants are really programming that last third.

SP: And it's kind of an unspoken pledge that we'll keep playing a film until everyone who wants to has seen it.

BP: Film exhibition is primarily, in my mind, the comfort of the patron. Are the sight lines good? You would be amazed how many theatres are designed with bad sight lines. I learned from ushering the importance of ventilation. It used to annoy my managers at Telluride that I would constantly be biking from venue to venue and feeling the air. Was it cool enough? Was the air moving fast enough? You can't imagine how quickly an audience tires if they don't have good airflow in the theatre. I've always had a pretty good sense of how bright the picture should be, what the right aspect ratio is, how you integrate a live introduction as smoothly as possible to the on-screen performance.

JR: *Could you talk about your relations with other festivals?*

BP: Competition with other festivals is significant. With the New York Film Festival, the rule is pretty simple; the opening night film at New York must be a North American première.

SP: Is it not true for the closing night film as well?

BP: Sometimes they try to press that.

SP: We have always had a really amicable relationship with New York. If we hear that they are seriously considering a film for opening night, we don't tear after it. I think it's still pretty edgy with Toronto. Periodically, they'd yell and scream at the distributors, 'You've played it at Telluride, we won't play it'. But most of the distributors say: 'It's going to play in Telluride, and then you can have it'. I think Venice has been an issue.

BP: It's more a question of timing, because we run at the same time as Venice. And they really do want the world première. But in some cases, we beat them to it.

SP: It's been a little bit of a downside for Telluride, because you'll actually see a film listed as premièred at a grand event like Toronto, when it actually played two weeks earlier in Telluride. Or you see 'worldwide première in Venice', when 24 hours earlier it played in Telluride. The bargain with the devil is that if we agree not to talk about premières, if we don't have grand soirées, then Venice says, 'OK, you can play it 24 hours earlier, but we had the world première'. Fine! I think the festival that provides the greatest pressure is Sundance. That pressure comes from distributors who play a film at Sundance and then, later in the year, want it to play at Telluride. We're pretty fearsome about that not happening. There have been a handful of exceptions over the years, sometimes depending on a tribute. We showed *Reservoir Dogs* [Quentin Tarantino, USA, 1992] for a tribute to Harvey Keitel, following its debut at Sundance. This is rare.

Festivity

JR: *Let's talk about the festive aspect, the ways in which Telluride is much more than a series of film screenings.*

BP: The really important thing about Telluride is that I don't think there's another festival where it takes over the entire town. The theatres are located in such a position that you can't get away from it. In Cannes, if you wanted to get away from the festival, in a few hundred yards you can. But Telluride is really like a film festival carnival. It's very festive, with flags flying from all the previous festivals.

SP: We have always tried to promote Telluride as a big party. For the Opening Night Feed — a gigantic meal for everybody — we'd lock down all of Main Street. We feed the pass-holders, because a happy, well-fed pass-holder is a happy person standing in line. And then there are three seminars in the park, one each day. That's a big thing because each day everyone comes together in the same place.

JR: *What's the role of the gondola, which ferries pass-holders up and down the mountain?*

SP: A gondola ride is like a mini-seminar. You know, eight people go up or down together for fifteen minutes. It's one of the best places to discuss

4.1 At the station in downtown Telluride, gondolas take festival goers to and from the Mountain Village, giving riders additional opportunities to discuss movies together. © Jeffrey Ruoff

the films. You can sit next to strangers. You can go up the gondola next to Clint Eastwood or come down next to Laura Linney (figure 4.1).

BP: When we set up the first Telluride festival, I just asked myself, 'How do I like to attend film festivals, not as a guest, but as a participant?' And when I thought about Filmex or San Francisco, I liked an intensive, three- or four-day period of time. After that, it became counter-productive: you were too tired to really enjoy yourself.

SP: We needed a three-day weekend in Telluride because you actually had to *go* to Telluride. It wasn't like in a city where you could work and then attend a festival screening in the evening.

BP: One of the genius ideas of the festival, developed totally by accident, was choosing Labour Day weekend, three days at the beginning of September. We realised it was the first major festival after Cannes. And of course, now, it fits in perfectly with everyone's Academy plans. The fall is when they start coming out with their Academy pictures.

JR: *When films are shown, they're presented and there's a conversation, there's something else that happens in addition to the screening. Tell me about that.*

BP: Well, it's a way to make it an experience, make it come alive with a three-dimensional aspect. We made it a requirement that the director be present. In some cases, we know that it's not realistic. But from the beginning, we required that somebody be there representing the film, usually the primary artist. And there's another purpose behind the policy. While that director is walking around the street, or riding in a gondola, audience members can talk to him about their film experience, and filmmakers love that. It's something that they don't usually get.

SP: Telluride is not a fan festival, so there are very little, if any, autograph issues. People don't rush up and say, 'Please sign my fingernails'.

JR: *For other kinds of screenings, you might have B. Ruby Rich, or Stan Brakhage, or Werner Herzog introduce the films or interview the directors. Why?*

SP: That's what we call our intelligence quotient. It's exciting to have interesting people talking to interesting people. You know, each theatre has an 'introducer'.

BP: A ringmaster.

SP: It's fascinating to watch Salman Rushdie interview a filmmaker. He has a specific way of looking at things, and so does the filmmaker. So you're really getting double bang for the buck. Think of the interview that Ebert did with Peter O'Toole.

BP: Oh, my god! That was magical.

SP: And at the end of the interview, they traded Keats quotes.

BP: Roger would start, and O'Toole would finish, then he'd give a line and Ebert would finish.

JR: *Telluride sounds like a community, a kind of a family, which is a term Herzog used to describe it. Could you talk about that aspect?*

SP: Look at the staff. The rate of return is huge. People come back year after year, and people get to know one another from all parts of the country. And then there is a real corps of people who come to produce the festival, the intelligence quotient of the festival, those people who do the interviews; it's the same people year after year.

BP: In the early years, the corps was Chuck Jones, Werner Herzog, Stan Brakhage, and Ken Burns. It's hard to imagine four more dissimilar people, yet there they were, year after year.

JR: *How did you come up with the idea of annual guest programmers?*

BP: When Bill Everson left, Tom and I decided to try replacing him with one-time guest directors. This was one of our best inventions. I think we started with the film critic Donald Richie. We've had wonderful guest directors such as filmmakers John Boorman, Errol Morris, Peter Bogdanovich, Edgardo Cozarinsky.

SP: Stephen Sondheim, the composer, was very good.

BP: Major player. Usually, Tom or I would say to the guest director, 'Think of a half-dozen programmes that you'd like to present'. One of the biggest risks was somebody I suggested, after I'd moved to Dartmouth: Peter Sellars, a New England legend. I'd never seen his work, but Tom thought that he was a great idea. Sellars turned out to be one of the best directors ever, and he comes back every year now. He's on the street and people get to talk with him.

SP: The critic John Simon was wonderful, smitten with Ingmar Bergman's muse, Harriet Andersson. She was a tribute guest and he was supposed to interview her on stage. He was dumbfounded. He didn't know what to say. He was acerbic to everyone else, in typical John Simon fashion, but I think he loved being a guest director.

BP: From the beginning, we thought the guest director should be a person who could bring other arts to Telluride; a musician, a visual artist. We tried to expand the view of what a film lover could be. We've had authors — Don DeLillo, Guillermo Cabrera Infante. They really put a stamp of quality on the festival.

Periodisation

JR: *In retrospect, would you divide Telluride up into separate periods, three or four different eras?*

SP: There were the pre-1979 years, sort of halcyon years, when the festival was small, when it was just hanging in there financially.

BP: 1979, in addition to the landmark revival of *Napoleon*, was the year that we were thinking about leaving Telluride. We had had enough of financially supporting the festival with our office help and our services. We didn't get any salaries, and it was taking more and more of our time, so we thought, 'Gee, let's move this baby to Aspen'.

SP: We had already written a National Endowment for the Arts grant to move to Aspen.

BP: And we'd written the press release!

SP: But the ski area and the town of Telluride got the word — 'rumble, rumble, they're going away', and the owner of the ski area came to us and said, 'You can't leave, and I will give you a lot of money if you stay'. So, after 1979, we had more financial backing. We still didn't get paid, but we did pay our key people a pittance. What, going from 1979 forward, was the next big change?

BP: The première of *My Dinner with Andre* [Louis Malle, USA, 1981].

SP: You think that made a difference in being able to get bigger pictures?

BP: Yes. We recognised the importance of a world première. *My Dinner with Andre* was a big, big hit. It was offered to us by Louis Malle, and we heard afterwards that it made Richard Roud of the New York Film Festival really unhappy.

SP: Andre Gregory and Wally Shawn, who play themselves in the film, came. They were very much part of the New York art world and that helped to expand us out there. That year, 1981, was also the year that Keith Carradine came riding in to the festival on his motorcycle. He was the very first Hollywood dude to build a house in Telluride. The door to the town was opened to the Hollywood population.

JR: *In the 1980s, what happened to expand the festival and put it on more solid footing?*

BP: After a decade of running the festival, we still weren't getting paid for our work. It was around 1985, I think, when it suddenly occurred to us that it would be good if that changed. The town of Telluride was taking off like crazy, in terms of being a ski area. And everything was getting more expensive.

SP: One of the horrible anomalies about dealing with this event is that, in being a ski area, Telluride has different rates for different times of the year.

The Telluride film festival is a high-season week. A room that would have cost $200 now costs $950. And the irony was that they would charge *us* $950 to put our guests in those rooms. Anyway, in the mid-1980s, we hired somebody to fundraise for us on a full-time basis.

BP: We decided to grow the festival. Telluride has sold out every single year since its beginning. We knew we could sell the seats, so we built another 500-seat theatre, converting a gym into what became The Max. This literally doubled, overnight, the number of passes that could be sold. And that had a huge effect. More recently, in 1999, we built the Chuck Jones theatre on the mountain, adding another 500 seats. These theatres were necessary to bring the festival into economic solvency.

SP: And then there was the Galaxy.

BP: The Galaxy, another 500 seats. So we went from a festival with around 800 seats to one with 2,600 seats. All of this growth was wanted and, we felt, needed. It made it possible to pay the airfares of the guests.

JR: *How did the Pence family make the transition from Colorado to Hanover, New Hampshire?*

SP: Well, it was pretty easy, I guess. We were living half in Colorado, half in Santa Fe. We had recently sold our distribution company, so we began to think about the possibility of moving East and about different things in film that we had and hadn't done. Neither of us was interested in production, so the next thing was academia. Shelton Stanfill, who was the director of the Hopkins Center for the Arts at Dartmouth College at that time, was a good friend of ours from Telluride. He told us, 'I think there is an opening for a position in film here, why don't you apply?' So Bill did, and we picked up and moved when he got the job. We continued our work on Telluride from the East Coast.

BP: There was another transformation at Telluride around the time of *Lost in Translation* [Sofia Coppola, USA/Japan, 2003], which was ...

SP: ... kind of the entry into the blockbuster period. Over the last 10 years or so Telluride has been hot for the next Oscar picture. It's a blessing and a curse. It's the Faustian bargain.

BP: Now, everybody's sweating bullets that they won't be able to top *The King's Speech*. [Tom Hooper, 2010, UK] Well, they probably won't be able to top *The King's Speech*.

SP: And before that it was *Slumdog Millionaire* [Danny Boyle, UK, 2008] in 2008, before that *Juno* [Jason Reitman, USA, 2007], *Brokeback Mountain* [Ang Lee, USA/Canada, 2005] in 2005, *Girl with a Pearl Earring* [Peter Webber, UK/Luxembourg, 2003]. Naturally, the audience has changed. It's very expensive to go to Telluride. The demographic is quite wealthy. Many are there because they want to be the first ones to see *The King's Speech*. So we have fewer and fewer die-hard cinéphiles who are making the trek.

BP: Now there is an awareness of Telluride — particularly on the part of producers and distributors — as the launching pad of Academy Award kind of stuff. *The Last King of Scotland* [Kevin Macdonald, UK, 2006] was part of that trend. Since that time, there has always been at least one picture that became important in the Academy Awards cycle.

SP: And now it's expected. People are assuming that Telluride will have its finger on what the next Academy Awards stuff will be.

JR: *What do you think the future of a festival like Telluride is in a world where everyone has mobile devices for watching movies and everybody can watch films on Netflix?*

BP: Well, I think your introduction [to *Coming Soon to a Festival Near You: Programming Film Festivals*] makes a case for festivals becoming increasingly important.

SP: I am less inclined to go see *Casablanca* [Michael Curtiz, USA, 1942] on the big screen, when I can go see it on our own 47-inch at home. But I think for the communal experience of watching films, festivals may be the only way that we have left.

BP: There will always be a New York Film Festival.

SP: Always. And I think that for a city like Seattle, where it is important for a film festival to bring stuff that will never come otherwise, it will sustain.

JR: *Why, in 2006, did you leave Telluride?*

BP: 33 years is a long time. There's very little additional change that we felt we could effect. We were getting the rare films that we wanted, we were getting the Academy Award kind of attention. It sort of seemed like, where could you go from there? Telluride was at the top.

SP: Also, our daughters referred to Telluride as the third sibling. Their lives were constantly affected by the festival, as were ours. They grew up with this phantom sibling in their lives, which is not a bad thing. I don't want to make it sound like an onerous thing, because it was a lot of excitement for them to be a part of it. But it was so all-consuming for us — we ate, drank, and slept the film festival. We worked all day in the office. Then we'd go home and screen two or three movies. I mean, it was absolutely all-consuming, and 33 years of all-consuming is really all-consuming. So it finally just became time to do other things.

Note

1   This interview was originally published in Jeffrey Ruoff (ed.) *Coming Soon to a Festival Near You: Programming Film Festivals*. St Andrews: St Andrews Film Studies, 135-54.

Chapter 5
Revival on the Mountain:
The Politics of Cinematic Rediscovery at the Telluride Film Festival.
Tom Luddy, Festival Co-Founder and Co-Director, Interviewed by Brigitta B. Wagner[1]

Brigitta B. Wagner: *What did the American festival landscape look like in 1974, and what kind of contribution did you, Bill and Stella Pence, and James Card hope to make?*

Tom Luddy: There were only a few other film festivals then: the Chicago Film Festival, the New York Film Festival, the San Francisco Film Festival — which was the oldest one and with which I was very much involved — and a [now defunct] festival in L.A. called Filmex, run by Gary Essert and Gary Abrahams, colleagues of mine and Bill's.

My mentor in life and work was an African-American man named Albert Johnson, who lived in Berkeley and was on the programming committee of the San Francisco Film Festival in the early 1960s and then, from the mid-1960s through the early 1970s, was its artistic director. The San Francisco Film Festival inspired Bill and me. When Bill was working at Janus Films, he used to come out to the festival, where I assisted Albert Johnson. What Bill and I loved about the festival was something that Johnson had innovated: making tributes to great figures from film history a central part of the event. Other film festivals at the time were focussed on showing new films and did not have anything like what we were doing in San Francisco, where we would have Busby Berkeley in person, Howard Hawks in person, Vincente Minnelli in person, Raoul Walsh in person, Leo McCarey in person. We would also have producers like Jack Warner. Legendary people. We would show clips, have a conversation with them, and even screen nitrate prints in their entirety.

When Bill and I started Telluride with James Card, we wanted to make tributes, retrospectives and revivals central to the festival. Albert had had me programme a whole F. W. Murnau series for San Francisco, and we had gotten all the great prints from Germany. In the 1960s, I had also done a [Aleksandr] Dovzhenko retrospective for which we got

Dovzhenko's widow. San Francisco was our inspiration, and we were following in that tradition. In the first years, we brought Albert, who was a great expert on musicals, to Telluride to present programmes of rare musical films. And given that James Card was at the George Eastman House and that I was at the Pacific Film Archive, it was natural for us to root the festival in celebrating the history of cinema.

BW: *The other festivals you mentioned were in major US cities. How did you come to choose Telluride, a tiny and remote mining town in the Rockies, as your location?*

TL: Bill was at Janus Films, which later became Criterion. At the time, Janus had a very large business in 16mm non-theatrical distribution; it also had 35mm distribution to all the repertory cinemas across the country (quite a few in those days) as well as to cinémathèques. Bill was in charge of their 35mm theatrical distribution and although their office was in New York, he persuaded Janus to let him move to Colorado and run the 35mm distribution business from Denver with the help of Stella and a few others. Bill always loved (and still does) having movie theatres to programme, and he took over a theatre in Denver. I booked a lot of films myself from Janus, and back in New York in the 1960s, I had been the head of a rival distribution company, Brandon Films. So we had been colleagues way back then. Once Bill got rooted in Colorado, he started expanding beyond Denver and leasing venues in places like Vail and Aspen, where he would show films at the height of the ski season. At the time there was no DVD or video or anything, and he had a theatre he loved in Aspen. This was all around 1972–73.

Then he heard that skiing had just started in Telluride, a town with a really small population, and that there was a beautiful old opera house that could be available to him if he wanted to do the same thing he was doing in Aspen. He discovered Telluride that way and fell in love with it. He knew James Card, as I did, and brought him out to show a film from the Eastman House in Aspen. I think he also took Jim down to see Telluride's Sheridan Opera House and to screen a film for the few people who were there. Bill had no thought of ever starting a film festival in Telluride, but Jim, a very flamboyant character, said, 'This place is too special. This theatre is too special. Let's start a little film festival here that will show new and old films, and the person who should be our partner is Tom Luddy'.

BW: *And how did your alliance with James Card begin?*

TL: I had started at the Pacific Film Archive in 1972, basically right at the beginning. Henri Langlois was a big supporter of the archive and also a good friend of mine and of Jim's. He did not like the Museum of Modern Art in New York, and he wanted to build allies in the cinémathèque world outside of MoMA. So he was very supportive of the Pacific Film Archive. I got to know Jim through Langlois and went out to Rochester. Then I got Jim to come out to Berkeley for a three-month series called 'Treasures from the George Eastman House' — an amazing programme. He came for the first few weeks, and while he was at the Pacific Film Archive, he quickly saw that we were not just showing older films. All the New German filmmakers were running around along with Kurosawa [Akira], and he saw that I seemed to know everybody in the world. He also knew my work at the San Francisco Film Festival. So he said to Bill, 'The three of us can cover the waterfront'. They called me, and I flew out to Colorado. We met in Telluride, and I loved the place, too.

That is how we decided to cook up the Telluride Film Festival. It was a labour of love. We did not pay ourselves for 20 years and basically subsidised the festival through our other jobs. The Pacific Film Archive paid the phone bills and shipping, and I screened films in our theatres. When I left for American Zoetrope in 1980, Zoetrope paid the FedEx bills and shipping. Janus and later film programming at Dartmouth College were Bill's day jobs.

BW: *In the festival's first year you made a statement with some bold programming choices, such as silent film diva Gloria Swanson and German filmmaker Leni Riefenstahl, who had famously filmed the 1934 National Socialist Party rally in Nuremberg and the 1936 Nazi Olympics. As you adapted San Francisco's tributes to Telluride, did you have strong ideas of whom you wanted to pursue?*

TL: A lot of the silent filmmakers and actors were still alive. James Card was famous for having Louise Brooks at the George Eastman House, but by the time Telluride came about, he was on the outs with her, having been her lover. He wanted to bring Gloria Swanson instead because he had some of her best films, including *Sadie Thompson* [1928], which was missing the last reel, at the George Eastman House.

Because our festival was in the mountains, he also wanted to bring the greatest *Bergfilm* actress and filmmaker, Leni Riefenstahl, and to show *Die weiße Hölle vom Piz Palü* [*White Hell of Piz Palü*, Germany, 1929] and *Das blaue Licht* [*The Blue Light*, Germany, 1932]. It was rather controversial, but that was his choice.

Bill asked me to get some contemporary filmmakers. I was already friends with Francis [Ford] Coppola, so I invited him for a tribute in the first year. At the time, I was basically supporting Kenneth Anger, who was literally living with me and my wife in an extra room in our house. Kenneth was a film buff, so I brought him. I think I was also the one who brought Stan Brakhage. I was very good friends with Dušan Makavejev, who had been to the Archive, so I brought him the first year. We liked the mix of experimental and contemporary films.

Henri Langlois also wanted to put his stamp on Telluride in the very first year to show, 'I am behind these people'. Though he could not come, he sent us a programme called 'Treasures from the Cinémathèque Française'. He was not sending a programme like that to New York. He chose to support us that way, and he helped us get one or two French films that we showed that year, too.

BW: *What were the reactions to the first Telluride programme? What kind of audience did you attract?*

TL: In the first and second years, we announced the programme in advance. *The New York Times* actually covered the festival. I think in general people fell in love with the concept. In what we called the 'world of specialised film exhibition' in those days, everybody knew everybody else. Bill and I especially knew anybody in any city that had an art theatre or repertory cinema. I had run movie theatres and been a distributor and was always sharing prints from the Pacific Film Archive with cinémathèque programmes and repertory art theatres. Janus Films had a huge collection — all the Bergman films and French classics — and Bill was the person people contacted if they wanted a film for their theatres in Winston-Salem, or Tampa, or L.A.

In those days there were wonderful, independent exhibitors who were not part of a chain. Every city had somebody who had a great art theatre and a passion for cinema — Ted Pedas in Washington, Randy Findley in Seattle, Max and Bob Laemmle in L.A., Elliott Wilhelm in Detroit, The Orson Welles Cinema in Boston. We knew them all. We said to them, 'We want to convene a film festival. Here is what we are doing. Why don't you guys come?' This group from across the country was the core, and they came again and again. Some of them are still coming, though not too many are left.

BW: *In Telluride lore, 1979, the year you screened Abel Gance's* Napoleon *in triptych, looms large. I have heard the story of Gance sitting in the Sheridan Hotel, where we are now [2012], watching the outdoor projection across the street. How did you manage to get the film, then being restored by Kevin Brownlow, and Gance to Colorado?*

TL: I always had a thing for Abel Gance. In the early 1960s, in my early twenties, I used to screen excerpts of *Napoleon*, which you could find on 16mm, to my film societies. I also screened 16mm prints of *La roue* [*The Wheel*, France, 1923] and *Un grand amour de Beethoven* [*The Life and Loves of Beethoven*, France, 1936]. I knew Nelly Kaplan's documentary *Abel Gance, hier et demain* [*Abel Gance: Yesterday and Tomorrow*, France, 1963], which had clips from *Napoleon*, so I was always obsessed with the film. When I was at the Pacific Film Archive, I presented *Napoleon* in 1973 and 1975 in a San Francisco theatre that had a Wurlitzer organ. I got the prints — Kevin's first restoration and the next one that was a bit further along — from the British Film Institute. Because the Pacific Film Archive's theatre only had 200 seats, we rented a larger one and put up three screens. Chris Reyna, who works here at Telluride, was our projectionist. Francis Coppola came to the screening in 1975 and went crazy for the film. I had always wanted to see if we could get Abel Gance to Telluride with the film, though we did not have an organ and couldn't have an orchestra.

Kevin Brownlow told Bill and me that Gance would never be able to travel, that he was living with some people in Nice and was in his late eighties and very frail. He thought it was not worth pursuing, but we said, 'We never take no for an answer'. Somehow we were able to find out the name of the family that was caring for him. So Bill and I and Annette Insdorf, who spoke good French, all took a side trip during the Cannes Film Festival to go visit him. He was rather frail but said, 'I'd rather die on a trip to Colorado than stay here like a vegetable'.

BW: *Though film archivists would have known the film, how well known was it in repertory circles and beyond?*

TL: The film was not available to be shown in repertory cinemas, but the Berkeley people knew about the film and Abel Gance. The American Film Institute in Washington also showed the film once or twice in the 1970s. I'm not sure about New York. Also in the 1970s, Claude Lelouch bought the rights to *Napoleon*, so that Gance could make a sound film called *Bonaparte et la révolution* [*Bonaparte and the Revolution*, France, 1972]. In that film Gance combined some of the material from *Napoleon* with some new material that he shot. That film was picked up for distribution by Robert A. Harris, who is now a major film restorer. In those days Bob had a distribution company called Images Film Archive, and he bought the American distribution rights to *Bonaparte et la révolution*, which even showed at the New York Film Festival. So Gance was known in film festival circles, and a sound version of *Napoleon* had actually shown in New York

5.1 The climatic triptych appears at the end of *Napoleon*, during its celebrated open-air projection at the 1979 Telluride film festival, with director Abel Gance present. © Philip Borgeson

and the Pacific Film Archive. There was awareness. Then Gance actually came to Telluride, and we showed *Napoleon* in Elks Park with a piano. It was unforgettable, one of the high points for Telluride (figure 5.1).

BW: *In 1978, the year before this screening, film scholars got together in Brighton, England, to talk about taking early cinema more seriously, for example, in the way that they looked at films, understood the development of film form, and wrote film history. In the academic world the Brighton Conference was a turning point in reconsidering the silent era as a serious area of study, but also in creating a new awareness among students to know these films and seek them out. How did Telluride's screening of* Napoleon *affect popular interest in silent cinema?*

TL: Even before *Napoleon*, we turned people on to early silent cinema. We not only had stars and filmmakers from the 1920s, but also even earlier. One of the first movie stars, Viola Dana, who was already acting in films in the early 1910s, was our guest in 1976. We also had Ben Carré, who was 93 at the time, as a tribute in 1977. He had been Maurice Tourneur's art director from the mid-1910s to about 1925, so we showed *The Blue Bird* [USA, 1918] and many classic films. Hal Roach, who had started out making two-reel films with Harold Lloyd, came in 1978, so we were able to celebrate very early silent film well before *Napoleon*.

BW: *But your personal efforts to introduce* Napoleon *to a broader public did not end with the Telluride screening.*

TL: I think our screening of *Napoleon* helped, but what created the most awareness was when Francis Coppola, together with Bob Harris, bought the rights to the film. I was working for Coppola then, and we commissioned his father, Carmine Coppola, to do an orchestral score. Then we brought *Napoleon* with a full live symphony orchestra to Radio City Music Hall in New York in 1981, and we sold out performance after performance. Then we went on the road with the film for two years in every city in America. There were ten screenings in L.A. in a 6,000-seat venue. Everybody who was anybody was there. Leonard Bernstein was in the audience in New York. Gloria Swanson was in the audience in New York.

BW: *So you were presenting silent cinema as high art, much like going to the opera?*

TL: Yes. Never before in America had silent films been shown outside of the world of film buff, cinémathèque, museum, and festival environments. *Time* called it the 'show business event of the year'. Abel Gance was still alive and could not come, but he kept in touch via phone. This event created interest in having live musical accompaniment, in silent cinema's greatness, in having other silent films shown theatrically and in saving movie palaces. Sophisticated New Yorkers in those days never went to Radio City Music Hall because they associated it with the Rockettes. We made them rediscover Radio City Music Hall and in other cities we took over theatres that were about to go out of business, like the Chicago Theatre and the Atlanta Fox. So many people came to *Napoleon* screenings in those cities that they really began to think about restoring these theatres and keeping them alive for cultural purposes.

We also took *Napoleon* abroad and showed it outside, against the Colosseum in Rome. We took it to Tokyo, Berlin, Holland, Canada and Australia. Hundreds of thousands of people saw *Napoleon* with live music. At one point we had three different conductors touring the world with the film. I hired Chapin Cutler [who also works at Telluride] to be technical director for *Napoleon* tours in every city.

BW: *In addition to increasing the awareness of international film heritage,* Napoleon *must have generated enormous profits. Did any of this flow back into restoration and preservation efforts?*

TL: Tragically, the *Napoleon* world tour was hugely expensive. We did not have any non-profit support from governments. There was some profit, but at the same time [Coppola] was making *One from the Heart* [USA, 1982] at Zoetrope's studio in L.A. The company went into near bankruptcy with that film. Francis was in debt for $20 million, and whatever we made from the *Napoleon* tour all went into that black hole.

BW: *But you had established a productive partnership between New Hollywood and film history. We might also think of filmmakers like Martin Scorsese's later efforts to promote the history of Italian cinema and the like.*

TL: Scorsese and every single one of them came to the *Napoleon* screenings, specifically in New York and L.A. Scorsese was all over the place. Francis and his father were totally behind my project. Coppola was the first contemporary director to really do this.

BW: *How do you go about making programme selections for silent films?*

TL: Well, Paolo [Cherchi Usai] has *carte blanche* with one programme called 'Pordenone Presents', and usually I come up with something. There are still so many unknown treasures from the silent era that we plan to show. I told Gary Meyer, my co-director, 'There are screenings of Carl Theodor Dreyer's *La Passion de Jeanne d'Arc* [*The Passion of Joan of Arc*, France, 1928] all the time, but nobody's seen Marco de Gastyne's film *La Merveilleuse vie de Jeanne d'Arc* [*Saint Joan the Maid*, France/Germany, 1929]. Let's show it'. Gary took a look at the film and thought it would be a good idea. I also told Paolo. Now even though it was not his programme, I always want Paolo to be supportive of anything we do with silent films. I do not think he had seen the film. I showed it to him, and he thought it would be a great idea. [In this year's 'Pordenone Presents'] Paolo's going to show Clarence Badger's *Hands Up!* [USA, 1926] with Raymond Griffiths, a silent comedian who is not as well known as Chaplin, Keaton, and Lloyd, but should be.

BW: *Would some of these other festivals like Pordenone's Le Giornate del Cinema Muto or Bologna's Il Cinema Ritrovato have been possible without a Telluride?*

TL: I think so. The Cinémathèque Française, the British Film Institute, the Museum of Modern Art in New York are really the granddaddies of everyone. With MoMA it goes back to the 1930s. They were not film festivals, but they were archives doing all this work.

When we started doing this in the 1970s and early 1980s, there were not many others in the festival world promoting silent film. Now everybody is doing it. We are just one of the group. There is the San Francisco Silent Film Festival, which is fantastic. There is Pordenone, and there is Bologna, which is probably the most important festival now for revivals and rediscoveries. That is all they do; much more so than we do.

BW: *So what is the difference that a film festival, and Telluride in particular, can make to this culture of preservation and rediscovery?*

TL: A film festival brings in a real cinéphile audience, can usually afford to bring guests in person and gives film a high profile. Because of James Card, we invited, from the very beginning, some famous archivists like Jacques Ledoux from the Cinémathèque Royale de Belgique. In 1978, he brought *Miss Mend* [*The Adventures of the Three Reporters*, USSR, 1926] by the Soviet director Boris Barnet, who later got discovered in Pordenone.

It was always our goal to show silent and archival films in the way they were meant to be seen: on 35mm, with live music, with an audience, a group experience, with perfect aperture plates and frame size. In the early days, we were even able to show nitrate prints here. We can provide a theatrical experience for a group of people in a movie theatre, which is different from looking at a film at home on DVD. With live music, too. We helped put the Alloy Orchestra on the map the first time we had them at Telluride.

We also created a great awareness of *Lonesome* [USA, 1928] by Paul Fejos [Pál Fejös]. We showed it two or three times over the years. The George Eastman House has the only print. Filmmakers who were at Telluride were blown away by it, and the film is finally coming out as a Criterion DVD. We have helped a lot of silent films this way because everybody is here: critics like Leonard Maltin, and so on. We started a whole new life for certain older films, at least on the festival circuit.

Brigitta B. Wagner is a film historian, filmmaker, and curator living in Berlin. She is the editor of *DEFA after East Germany* (2014), the author of *Berlin Replayed* (2015), and the director of *Rosehill* (2015). She attended and worked for the Telluride Film Festival from 2000 to 2015 and is now a member of Berlin cinema collective WOLF Kino.

Notes

1   This interview took place on 30 August 2012, the day before the opening of the 39th Telluride Film Festival, in the Sheridan Hotel, from which the ageing Abel Gance had watched a screening of *Napoleon* over three decades earlier. It was originally published in *Film Festival Yearbook 5: Archival Film Festivals*, Alex Marlow-Mann (ed.), St Andrews: St Andrews Film Studies, 233-42.

Festivals Cited

Berlin International Film Festival, http://www.berlinale.de/en/HomePage.
html

Buenos Aires International Festival of Independent Cinema, http://
festivales.buenosaires.gob.ar/es/bafici

Busan International Film Festival, http://www.biff.kr

Cannes Film Festival, http://www.festival-cannes.com/en.html

Chicago International Film Festival, http://www.chicagofilmfestival.com

Cork Film Festival, http://www.corkfilmfest.org

Ebertfest: Roger Ebert's Film Festival, http://www.traversecityfilmfest.
org/about/

Edinburgh International Film Festival, http://www.edfilmfest.org.uk

Filmex, 1971–83, no website

Full Frame Documentary Film Festival, http://www.fullframefest.org

Hong Kong International Film Festival, http://www.hkiff.org.hk/en/index.
php

Il Cinema Ritrovato, http://www.ilcinemaritrovato.it

International Film Festival Rotterdam, http://www.filmfestivalrotterdam.
com/en

Jeonju International Film Festival, http://eng.jiff.or.kr

Karlovy Vary International Film Festival, http://www.kviff.com/en/news/

Locarno Film Festival, http://www.pardo.ch/jahia/Jahia/home/lang/en

Midnight Sun Film Festival, http://www.msfilmfestival.fi/index.php/en/

Mill Valley Film Festival, http://www.mvff.com

Montreal World Film Festival, http://www.ffm-montreal.org/en/home.
html

New York Film Festival, http://www.filmlinc.com/pages/new-york-film-
festival

New York African Film Festival, http://www.africanfilmny.org

Ottawa International Animation Festival, http://www.animationfestival.
ca

Pesaro Film Festival, http://www.pesarofilmfest.it/?lang=en

Pordenone Silent Film Festival, http://www.cinetecadelfriuli.org/gcm/

Robert Flaherty Film Seminar, http://www.flahertyseminar.org

San Francisco International Film Festival, http://www.sffs.org/sf-intl-film-
festival.aspx

San Francisco Silent Film Festival, http://www.silentfilm.org

Sundance Film Festival, http://www.sundance.org/festival

TCM Classic Film Festival, http://filmfestival.tcm.com

Telluride Film Festival, http://www.telluridefilmfestival.org

Toronto International Film Festival, http://www.tiff.net/thefestival

TCM Classic Film Festival, http://filmfestival.tcm.com
Traverse City Film Festival, http://www.traversecityfilmfest.org/about/
Venice International Film Festival, http://www.labiennale.org/en/
    cinema/festival

Works Cited

Adams, Sam (2007) 'New team won't tamper with Telluride', *The Hollywood Reporter*, 29 August. On-line. Available HTTP: http://www.hollywoodreporter.com/news/new-team-wont-tamper-telluride-149012 (26 January 2015).

Altman, Rick (2004) *Silent Film Sound*. New York: Columbia University Press.

Andrews, David (2013) 'Art Cinema as Institution, Redux: Art Houses, Film Festivals, and Film Studies', *Theorizing Art Cinemas: Foreign, Cult, Avant-Garde, and Beyond*. Austin: University of Texas Press, 172–90.

Andrews, Rena (1974a) 'Coppola, Swanson Headline Telluride Film Fest', *The Denver Post*, 26 July, 78.

____ (1974b) 'Protest Clouds Movie Awards', *The Denver Post*, 3 September, 19.

____ (1974c) 'The Telluride Film Festival', *The Denver Post*, 4 September, 61–2, 64.

____ (1974d) 'Hitler's Favorite Filmmaker Honored at Colorado Festival', *The New York Times*, 15 September, 1D.

Anger, Kenneth (1975) *Hollywood Babylon*. San Francisco: Straight Arrow Books.

Appelo, Tim (2013a) 'Telluride: World's First Screening of "Prisoners" Leaves Audience Stunned', *The Hollywood Reporter*, 30 August. On-line. Available HTTP: http://www.hollywoodreporter.com/news/telluride-worlds-first-screening-prisoners-618623 (16 June 2014).

____ (2013b) 'Telluride: THR/UCLA TFT Party Attracts Everyone From Penn Jillette to Ralph Fiennes', *The Hollywood Reporter*, 31 August. On-line. Available HTTP: http://www.hollywoodreporter.com/news/telluride-thr-ucla-tft-party-618834 (27 January 2015).

Backstage (2004) 'NewsWire…', 10 November, On-line. Available HTTP: http://www.backstage.com/news/newswire_155 (26 January 2015).

Barbour, Elizabeth and the Telluride Historical Museum (2006) *Images of America: Telluride*. Arcadia Publishing: Charleston, SC.

Barsam, Richard (1974) 'Happily to hell you ride', *Village Voice*, 19 September, 86.

Bluetent (2013) 'From Hockey Rink to World Premiere-Worthy Cinema', *The Watch*, 28 August, On-line. Available HTTP: http://www.thewatchmedia.com/from-hockey-rink-to-world-premiere-worthy-cinema (26 January 2015).

Boxoffice (1974a) '2nd Telluride Film Festival Is Planned', 16 September, W6, W8.

_____ (1974b) 'Telluride Festival Draws Mixed Reviews by Critics', 23 September, W2-3.

Brody, Meredith (2013) 'Telluride Film Festival XL Launches Werner Herzog Theatre, 'Under the Sun', 'All is Lost', *Indiewire*, 2 September. On-line. Available HTTP: http://blogs.indiewire.com/thompsononhollywood/telluride-film-festival-xl-day-one (16 June 2014).

Cagin, Seth (2013) 'Why Five Days of Movie Pleasure Are Better Than Four', *The Watch*, 4 September, 4, 33.

Card, James (1999 [1994]) *Seductive Cinema: The Art of Silent Film*. Minneapolis: University of Minnesota Press.

Cowie, Peter (2010) *The Berlinale, The Festival*. Berlin: Bertz + Fischer.

Czach, Liz (2004) 'Film Festivals, Programming, and the Building of a National Cinema', *The Moving Image*, 4, 1, 76–88.

Darbonne, Rodger (1974) 'Impact at the Impasse: The Devil at Telluride', *Filmmakers Newsletter*, December, 69–70.

Dayan, Daniel (1997) 'In Quest of a Festival', *National Forum*, 77, 4, 41–7.

_____ (2000) 'Looking for Sundance: The Social Construction of a Film Festival', in Ib Bondebjerg (ed.) *Moving Images, Culture and the Mind*. Luton: Luton University Press, 43–52.

Deep Creek Review (1974) 'The Empty Chair: Leni's Seminar', September, 9.

Daily Sentinel (1974) 'Telluride fest attracts international celebrities', 6 August.

de Valck, Marijke and Skadi Loist (2009) 'Film Festival Studies: An Overview of a Burgeoning Field' in Dina Iordanova with Ragan Rhyne (eds) *Film Festival Yearbook 1: The Festival Circuit*. St Andrews: St Andrews Film Studies with College Gate Press, 179–215.

de Valck, Marijke (2012) 'Finding Audiences for Festivals: Programming in Historical Perspective', in Jeffrey Ruoff (ed.) *Coming Soon to a Festival Near You: Programming Film Festivals*. St Andrews: St Andrews Film Studies, 25–40.

Debruge, Peter (2013) 'Can Telluride Continue to Steal Venice and Toronto's Thunder?', *Variety*, 3 September. On-line. Available HTTP: http://variety.com/2013/film/news/telluride-film-festival-wrap-2013-oscars-1200596759 (16 June 2014).

Duffy, Mary (2012) 'Flashback to the Seventies', *Telluride Tales: Journal of the Telluride Historical Museum* v. 1, n. 1, Telluride, CO: Telluride Historical Museum, 3.

Durango-Coast Herald (1974) 'Telluride is transformed into Celluloid City', 8 September, 11.

Ebert, Roger (1974) 'Hue and cry about Leni continues', *Chicago Sun-Times*, 29 September, 1, 4, 6.

Elsaesser, Thomas (2005) 'Film Festival Networks: The New Topographies of Cinema in Europe', in Thomas Elsaesser, *European Cinema: Face to Face with Hollywood*. Amsterdam: Amsterdam University Press, 82–107.

English, James (2008) *Economies of Prestige: Prizes, Awards, and the Circulation of Cultural Value*. Cambridge: Harvard University Press.

Everson, William (1978) *American Silent Film*. New York: Oxford University Press.

Falassi, Alessandro (1987) *Time Out of Time: Essays on the Festival*. Albuquerque, NM: University of New Mexico Press.

Feinberg, Scott (2013a) 'Telluride: Robert Redford, Coppolas Dazzle Fellow Filmmakers at Opening Brunch', *The Hollywood Reporter*, 29 August. On-line. Available HTTP: www.hollywoodreporter.com/race/telluride-robert-redford-coppolas-dazzle-617614 (5 June 2014).

____ (2013b) 'Telluride: Steve McQueen's '12 Years a Slave' Met with Shock and Awe at World Premiere,' *The Hollywood Reporter*, 30 August. On-line. Available HTTP: http://www.hollywoodreporter.com/race/telluride-steve-mcqueens-12-years-618625 (26 January 2015).

Fetter, Richard L. and Suzanne Fetter (2001 [1979]) *Telluride: From Pick to Powder*. Caldwell, ID: Caxton Press.

Foundas, Scott (2012) 'The Future' in Laura Kern, Joanne Koch, and Richard Peña (eds), *New York Film Festival Gold: A 50th Anniversary Celebration*, New York: The Film Society of Lincoln Center, 110–13.

Gallo, William (1974a) 'First Telluride film festival Labor Day weekend', *Rocky Mountain News*, 28 July.

____ (1974b) 'Heated dispute and film glories unreel at Telluride', *Rocky Mountain News*, 8 September, 16.

____ (1974c) 'The Film Flap at Telluride Festival', *The Los Angeles Times*, 22 September.

Gluck, Marissa (2011) 'Telluride's Big Real Estate Listings', *The Hollywood Reporter (Pret-a-Reporter)*, 28 August. On-line. Available HTTP: http://www.hollywoodreporter.com/news/tellurides-big-real-estate-listings-227941 (27 January 2015).

Greenspun, Roger (2012) 'Old Times' in Laura Kern, Joanne Koch, and Richard Peña (eds), *New York Film Festival Gold: A 50th Anniversary Celebration*. New York: The Film Society of Lincoln Center, 44–7.

Grimes, William (1996) 'William K. Everson, Historian and Film Preservationist, 67', *The New York Times*, 16 April. On-line. Available HTTP: http://www.nytimes.com/1996/04/16/nyregion/william-k-everson-historian-and-film-preservationist-67.html (14 June 2014).

Hammond, Pete (2013) 'Telluride: Jason Reitman's "Labor Day" Debut', *Deadline Hollywood*, 30 August. On-line. Available HTTP: http://deadline.com/2013/08/telluride-jason-reitmans-labor-day-debut-575314 (27 January 2015).

Hernandez, Eugene (2013a) 'With "Prisoners" & "12 Years a Slave" in the Mix, Telluride Audiences Face Tough Choices', *Filmlinc Daily*, 29 August. On-line. Available HTTP: http://www.filmlinc.com/blog/entry/telluride-prisoners-jake-gyllenhaal-hugh-jackman-12-years-a-slave (16 June 2014).

____ (2013b) 'The View from Telluride: Previewing a New Season of Cinema', *Filmlinc Daily*, 4 September. On-line. Available HTTP: http://www.filmlinc.com/daily/entry/telluride-12-years-a-slave-gravity-under-the-skin-the-wind-rises (16 June 2014).

Horn, John (2013) 'Telluride Film Festival at 40: Many celebrants, some growing pains', *Los Angeles Times*, 29 August. On-line. Available HTTP: http://www.latimes.com/entertainment/envelope/moviesnow/la-et-mn-telluride-film-festival-20130829-story.html (16 June 2014).

Iordanova, Dina (2016a) 'Film Festivals and Film Culture's Transnational Essence', Preface to Marijke de Valck, Skadi Loist and Brendan Kredell (eds) *Film Festivals*. London and New York: Routledge (forthcoming).

____ (2016b) 'Yingying, Zhenzhen and Fenfen? China at the Festivals' in Berry, Chris and Luke Robinson (eds) *Chinese Film Festivals* (forthcoming).

Just Jared (2013) 'Brad Pitt & Michael Fassbinder: AMPAS Party in Telluride', 1 September. On-line. Available HTTP: http://www.justjared.com/2013/09/01/brad-pitt-michael-fassbender-ampas-party-in-telluride (27 January 2015).

Kern, Laura, Joanne Koch, and Richard Peña (eds) *New York Film Festival Gold: A 50th Anniversary Celebration*. New York: The Film Society of Lincoln Center.

Koehler, Robert (2009) 'Cinephilia and Film Festivals' in Richard Porton (ed.) *Dekalog: On Film Festivals*. London: Wallflower, 81–97.

____ (2013) 'Review of *Coming Soon to a Festival Near You: Programming Film Festivals*', *Cineaste*, Winter, 39, 1, 71–3.

Laffly, Tomris (2013) '40th Telluride Film Festival unveils big guns and sneak peeks into its 2nd day....', *Film Journal International*, 31 August. On-line. Available HTTP: http://54.86.207.106/40th-telluride-film-festival-unveils-big-guns-and-sneak-peeks-into-its-2nd-day (18 June 2014).

Lichtenstein, Grace (1975) 'Colorado Town Lures Youths With Sun, Scenery, and Bagels', *The New York Times*, 16 April, 40.

Lloyd, Matthew (2011) *How the Movie Brats Took Over Edinburgh: The Impact of Cinephilia on the Edinburgh International Film Festival, 1968–1990*. St Andrews: St Andrews Film Studies.

Loden, Frako (2011) 'Nonfiction at 9,000 Feet: Telluride Kicks off the Fall Fest Season', *Documentary*, September. On-line. Available HTTP: http://www.documentary.org/magazine/nonfiction-9000-feet-telluride-kicks-fall-fest-season (20 June 2014).

Lopate, Phillip (2012) 'The New York Film Festival: Its First 50 Years' in Laura Kern, Joanne Koch, and Richard Peña (eds), *New York Film Festival Gold: A 50th Anniversary Celebration*. New York: The Film Society of Lincoln Center, 15–41.

McCarthy, Todd (2013) 'Telluride: Big Premieres Outshine Retrospectives as Festival Throws Itself a Great 40th', *The Hollywood Reporter*, 2 September. On-line. Available HTTP: http://www.hollywoodreporter.com/news/telluride-big-premieres-outshine-retrospectives-619384 (17 June 2014).

McReynolds, Janet (1974) 'Telluride Film Festival', *Camera*, Boulder, CO, 8 September.

McCue, Michelle (2011), 'Academy Grants $50,000 to Telluride Film Festival', 31 August. On-line. Available HTTP: http://www.wearemoviegeeks.com/2011/08/academy-grants-50000-to-telluride-film-festival (25 January 2015).

Means, Sean P. 'Redford to receive Silver Medallion at Telluride Film Festival', *The Salt Lake Tribune*, 28 August. On-line. Available HTTP: http://www.sltrib.com/sltrib/blogsmoviecricket/56793739-66/festival-telluride-drama-redford.html.csp (27 January 2015).

Newsweek (1974) 'Misguided Genius', 16 September, 91.

Papadimitriou, Lydia, and Jeffrey Ruoff, eds. (2016) 'Film Festivals: Origins and Trajectories', guest-edited special issue of *New Review of Film and Television Studies*, London: Taylor & Francis, 14, 1, March, (forthcoming).

Peranson, Mark (2009) 'First You Get the Power, Then You Get the Money: Two Models of Film Festivals', in Richard Porton (ed.) *Dekalog 3: On Film Festivals*. London: Wallflower, 23–37.

Poland, David (2005) 'The Ultimate Indie Fest Teams with The Academy', *Movie City News*, 17 August. On-line. Available HTTP: http://moviecitynews.com/2005/08/the-ultimate-indie-fest-teams-with-the-academy (16 June 2014).

Pond, Steve (2013) 'Why Alexander Payne and the Coen Brothers are Skipping the Toronto Film Fest', *The Wrap*, 13 August. On-line. Available HTTP: http://www.thewrap.com/movies/column-post/why-alexander-payne-and-coen-brothers-are-skipping-toronto-film-fest-112036 (16 June 2014).

___ (2014) 'Toronto Film Festival to Studios: It's Telluride or Us', 28 January. On-line. Available HTTP: http://variety.com/2013/film/awards/venice-topper-reacts-to-telluride-encroachment-1200598609 (16 June 2014).

Quinn, Tom (2013) 'Morris Herzog', *Hollywood Elsewhere*, 1 September. On-line. Available HTTP: http://www.hollywood-elsewhere.com/2013/09/morris-herzog (16 June 2014).

Quintín (2009) 'The Festival Galaxy', in Richard Porton (ed.) *Dekalog 3: On Film Festivals*. London: Wallflower, 28–52.

Renold, Evelyn (1974) 'A Refuge in the Rockies for Films and Folks', *Coast*, December, 20–1.

Rich, B. Ruby (1998), 'Angst and Joy on the Women's Film Festival Circuit', *Chick Flicks: Theories and Memories of the Feminist Film Movement*. Durham, NC: Duke University Press, 29–39.

Roddick, Nick (2013 [2009]) 'Coming to a Server Near You: The Film Festival in the Age of Digital Reproduction (2005–2012)' in Dina Iordanova (ed.) *The Film Festival Reader*. St Andrews Film Studies, 173–89.

Ruoff, Jeffrey (2012a) 'Programming Film Festivals', in Jeffrey Ruoff (ed.) *Coming Soon to a Festival Near You: Programming Film Festivals*. St Andrews: St Andrews Film Studies, 1–21.

___ (2012b) 'Programming the Old and the New: Bill and Stella Pence on the Telluride Film Festival', in Jeffrey Ruoff (ed.) *Coming Soon to a Festival Near You: Programming Film Festivals*. St Andrews: St Andrews Film Studies, 135–54.

Ruoff, Jeffrey (ed.) (2012) *Coming Soon to a Festival Near You: Programming Film Festivals*. St Andrews: St Andrews Film Studies.

Ruoff, Jeffrey (2013a) Interview with Bill Pence and Stella Pence, 8 June Hanover, NH.

___ (2013b) Interview with Rick Brook, 26 August, Telluride, CO.
___ (2013c) Interviews with Jim Bedford, 28–29 August, Telluride, CO.
___ (2013d) Interview with Marc Cousins, 31 August, Telluride, CO.
___ (2013e) Interview with Marc McDonald, 1 September, Telluride, CO.
___ (2013f) Interview with Chris Robinson, 9 September, Hanover, NH.
___ (2013g) Interview with Werner Herzog, 18 September, Hanover, NH.
___ (2013h) Interview with Zoe Elton, 2 December, telephone.

___ (2013i) Interview with Linda Williams, 4 December, telephone.
___ (2013j) Interview with Michael Barker, 5 December, telephone.
___ (2013k) Interview with James Schamus, 13 November, telephone.
___ (2013l) Interview with Tom Luddy, 15 November, telephone.
___ (2013) Interview with Richard Peña, 21 November, telephone.
___ (2013m) Interview with Paolo Cherchi Usai, 12 December, telephone.
___ (2013n) Interview with Robert Gardner, 16 December, telephone.
___ (2013o) Interview with Annette Insdorf, 18 December, email.
___ (2013p) Interview with Phillip Lopate, 18 December, telephone.
___ (2013q) Interview with Howie Movshovitz, 19 December, telephone.
___ (2014a) Interview with Gary Meyer, 21 February, Berkeley, CA.
___ (2014b) Interview with Bill Pence and Stella Pence, 17 February, Hanover, NH.
Sackett, Heather (2013) 'The Nugget goes digital', *Telluride Daily Planet*, 21 August. On-line. Available HTTP: http://telluridenews.com/articles/2013/12/19/news/doc5213f9e91a6e8882822762.txt (19 June 2014).
Schamus, James (2012) 'See Here Now: Festival Red Carpets and the Cost of Film Culture', in Jeffrey Ruoff (ed.) *Coming Soon to a Festival Near You: Programming Film Festivals*. St Andrews: St Andrews Film Studies, 69–74.
Scott, A. O. (2013) 'In Mountain Air, Foresight (Maybe)', *The New York Times*, 2 September. On-line. Available HTTP: http://www.nytimes.com/2013/09/03/arts/at-telluride-festival-a-redford-solo-and-other-previews.html?pagewanted=all&_r=0 (17 June 2014).
Secrest, Clark (1974) 'Finest Hour Due Opera House', *The Denver Post*, July 28, 78.
Shuman, Kai (1974) '*Sweet Movie*', *The Straight Creek Journal*, 10–17 September, 10.
Shoff, Emily Brendler (2013) 'Telluride Film Festival: Todd McCarthy Talks #40', Telluride Inside… and Out, 26 August. On-line. Available HTTP: http://www.tellurideinside.com/2013/08/telluride-film-festival-todd-mccarthy-talks-40.html (26 January 2015).
Sontag, Susan (1975) 'Fascinating Fascism', *The New York Review of Books*, 6 February, 23–30.
___ (1996) 'The Decay of Cinema', *The New York Times Magazine*, 25 February, 60–1.
Staples, Nikki (1974) 'Hollywood in Telluride', *The Straight Creek Journal*, 10–17 September, 10.

Stone, Sasha (2013) 'Telluride Diary: We All Shine On', *Awards Daily*, 1 September. On-line. Available HTTP: http://www.awardsdaily.com/blog/2013/09/telluride-diary-we-all-shine-on (27 January 2015).

Stringer, Julian (2001) 'Global Cities and the International Film Festival Economy', in Mark Shiel and Tony Fitzmaurice (eds.) *Cinema and the City: Film and Urban Societies in a Global Context*. Malden, MA: Blackwell, 134–44.

____ (2003a) 'Neither One Thing Nor the Other: Blockbusters at Film Festivals', in Julian Stringer (ed.) *Movie Blockbusters*. New York: Routledge.

____ (2003b) 'Raiding the Archive: Film Festivals and the Revival of Classic Hollywood', in Paul Grainge (ed.) *Memory and Popular Film*. Manchester: Manchester University Press, 81–96.

____ (2008) 'Genre Films and Festival Communities: Lessons from Nottingham, 1991–2000', *Film International* 6, 4, 53–9.

Taillibert, Christel (2009) *Tribulations festivalières: Les festivals de cinéma et audiovisuel en France*. Paris: L'Harmattan.

Tapley, Kristopher (2013) 'Telluride: Penn and Teller's "Tim's Vermeer" Might Be the Breakout Hit of the Festival', 2 September. On-line. Available HTTP: http://www.hitfix.com/in-contention/telluride-penn-and-tellers-tims-vermeer-might-be-the-breakout-hit-of-the-festival (27 January 2015).

Telluride Film Festival (2014) *2013 Yearbook*. Telluride, CO: National Film Preserve, Ltd.

Telluride Tales: Journal of the Telluride Historical Museum (2012) 'Dreaming Up a Ski Area', Telluride, CO: Telluride Historical Museum, 1, 1, 4–5.

Telluride Times (1974a) 'Film Festival Plans Revealed', 6 June.

____ (1974b) 'Film Festival Confirms Three Stellar Names', 25 July, 1.

____ (1974c) 'Underground Films To Be Represented at Festival', 1 August, 9.

____ (1974d) 'Telluride Film Festival Sold Out', 15 August, 1.

____ (1979a) 'Pence confirms film festival location is still undecided', 25 January, 2, 15.

____ (1979b) 'Pence announces Telluride will host 6th film festival', 1 February.

The Straight Creek Journal (1974a) 'Coppola', 10–17 September, 9.

____ (1974b) 'Gloria Swanson', 10–17 September, 8.

____ (1974c) 'Riefenstahl', 10–17 September, 9.

Thompson, Anne (2013) 'Telluride and Toronto Winners and Losers: Who Came Out Ahead', *Indiewire: Thompson on Hollywood*, 16 September. On-line. Available HTTP: http://blogs.indiewire.com/thompsononhollywood/telluride-and-toronto-wrap-who-came-out-ahead (16 June 2014).

___ (2014) *The $11 Billion Year: From Sundance to the Oscars, an Inside Look at the Changing Hollywood System*. New York: HarperCollins.

Trinz, Bruce (1974) 'Riefenstahl a Storm Center at Telluride and Chi Film Fests', *Variety*, 11 September.

Turan, Kenneth (2001) *From Sundance to Sarajevo: Film Festivals and the World They Made*. Berkeley: University of California Press.

Variety (1974a) 'Colorado Film Fest Schedules Tribute to Leni Riefenstahl', July 30.

___ (1974b) 'Nazi-Tainted Riefenstahl Honoured by Colo. Fest But "T'aint Politics", It Sez Here', 7 August, 1, 52.

Viebrock, Susan (2013a) 'Telluride Film Festival 2013: No Pass? Don't Pass', *Telluride Inside… and Out*, 25 August. On-line. Available HTTP: http://www.tellurideinside.com/2013/08/telluride-film-festival-2013-no-pass-dont-pass.html (16 June 2014).

___ (2013b) 'A Few Ways the Telluride Film Festival Thanks Telluride', *Telluride Inside… and Out*, August 26. On-line. Available HTTP: http://www.tellurideinside.com/2013/08/a-few-ways-the-telluride-film-festival-thanks-telluride.html (16 June 2014).

Vivarelli, Nick (2013) 'Venice Film Festival Director Blasts Telluride for Sneak Peaks', *Variety*, September 4. On-line. Available HTTP: http://variety.com/2013/film/awards/venice-topper-reacts-to-telluride-encroachment-1200598609 (16 June 2014).

Wagner, Brigitta B. (2013) 'Revival on the Mountain: The Politics of Cinematic Rediscovery at the Telluride Film Festival. An Interview with Tom Luddy, Festival Co-Founder and Co-Director', in Alex Marlow-Mann (ed.) *Film Festival Yearbook 5: Archival Film Festivals*. St Andrews: St Andrews Film Studies, 233–42.

Webb, Michael (1974) 'Telluride's First Film Feat', *The Washington Post*, September 15, H2.

Wells, Jeffrey (2013) 'Sad and Ghastly', *Hollywood Elsewhere*, 30 August. On-line. Available HTTP: https://twitter.com/wellshwood/status/373653458143805440 (16 June 2014).

Wolf, Ron (1979) 'State's other film festival to expand', *The Straight Creek Journal*, May 10.

Wong, Cindy (2011) *Film Festivals: Culture, People, and Power on the Global Screen*. Rutgers, NJ: Rutgers University Press.

Wright, Celine (2013) 'Telluride Film Festival is a labor of love for its SHOWCorps', *The Los Angeles Times*, 23 August. On-line. Available HTTP: http://articles.latimes.com/2013/aug/23/entertainment/la-et-mn-ca-telluride-film-buffs-20130825 (19 June 2014).

Index

Films Need Festivals, Festivals Need Films

Series Editor: Dina Iordanova

Advisory Board: Chris Berry (London), Mark Cousins (Edinburgh), Marijke de Valck (Utrecht), James English (Philadelphia), Jean-Michel Frodon (Paris), Lee Yong-kwan (Busan), Richard Porton (New York).

Films need festivals: All films seek exposure and, for many films, festivals are among the few available platforms that give such exposure. Yet, the festival circuit is a platform that is insufficiently explored and remains poorly understood.

Festivals need films: Having come into existence once, film festivals have an insatiable need for new content. Festivals depend on films for their own survival, threading the fine line between opulence and obscurity.

Work published in this series will improve the understanding of the way film travels through the festival circuit. It seeks to highlight and untangle the dialectics of the two. Conceptually, the project is based on notions of transnationalism and dialogism. It will pay attention to peripheral yet significant phenomena and will bring about new insights by breaking down the concept of a single festival circuit into many smaller self-contained yet interlocking clusters.

The series will seek to capture the dynamics of global film festivals. It will be comprehensive in its geographical coverage, with examples not only from the West but also stretching as far as Latin America and Africa and acknowledging the key importance of Asia. It will seek to analyse the reasons for the proliferation of film festivals in some cultural contexts as opposed to their restrained advancement in others. It will seek to show the range of stakeholders and forces that shape the film festival in relationship to tourism, cultural diplomacy or various activist causes. It will explore management and political aspects and the so-called economies of prestige. Last but not least, it will explore the relentless invasion of the digital forms of distribution and how they change the game.

Be in touch if you would like to discuss your proposal, please find the template for your book proposal here: http://www.st-andrews.ac.uk/globalcinema/publishing/information-for-authors/